MARKETER: A Simulation
Second Edition

MARKETER: A SIMULATION
Second Edition

Jerald R. Smith
University of Louisville

Peggy A. Golden
University of Louisville

Published to accompany *Marketing, Fifth Edition*,
by William M. Pride and O.C. Ferrell

Houghton Mifflin Company Boston
Dallas Geneva, Illinois Lawrenceville, New Jersey Palo Alto

Cover Photography: Martin Paul

Printed in the U.S.A.

ISBN: 0-395-42546-8

ABCDEFGHIJ-B-8987

CONTENTS

PREFACE

MARKETER: A Simulation is a dynamic business exercise designed for
students enrolled in any type of course that features the concepts of marketing. It provides student players with simulated real-world experience in
marketing decision making, and enables them to see the relevance and
application of the principles being taught in the course. The scenario and
rules of the simulation can be learned in only an hour, yet the simulation
contains all of the major concepts of marketing. An additional benefit for
players of *MARKETER* is the fact that early in the educational process
they will experience how the various areas of marketing mesh together and
affect one another. Although the scenario described in the student manual
is one concerning the home entertainment industry, the instructor can easily
substitute other scenarios.

In playing the simulation, students acting as management teams make a
variety of decisions that have an impact on their company's operations.
The decisions that each team must make concern pricing the product, advertising, sales promotion, sales force size and compensation, product development, marketing channels, and production levels. A unique and optional
feature of *MARKETER* is the inclusion of marketing environment and social
responsibility incidents that the firm faces in each decision period. Student
decisions are recorded on decision forms and can be analyzed and evaluated
quickly by a computer. The instructor needs no computer knowledge to
administer the simulation.

These are the objectives of *MARKETER: A Simulation*:

1. To allow students with different academic interests to make marketing
   mix decisions and to consider the multidimensional aspects of these
   decisions
2. To provide the opportunity for student interaction in organization
   teamwork
3. To improve the students' communication, leadership, and interpersonal
   relation skills

4. To help students develop rational decision-making skills
5. To demonstrate the importance of such management tools as budgeting, forecasting, strategic planning, breakeven and other types of data analyses
6. To introduce students to various marketing environmental, ethical, and social responsibility problems that may occur in a firm and to show the consequences of the decisions they make

Unfortunately, no simulation can duplicate real life. This simulation, however, attempts to build a marketing model that is as close as possible to actual conditions. It is suggested that student teams approach the simulation as a real-world environment in which they must compete against other firms, not "play against" the computer.

The administrator's instructions have been entered on the floppy disk. They explain how to administer the simulation and provide suggestions for grading the performance of student teams. A floppy disk is also provided for analyzing and evaluating student decisions. Suggestions concerning the simulation are always welcome.

ACKNOWLEDGEMENTS

To Distinguished Professor W. Stamm, who has always been an inspiration and role model. To Carl T. Eakin, ex-professor/dean-turned-businessman, who first suggested that I try writing a simulation for the classroom. To Distinguished Professor Richard Barber, who immersed me in business ethics. To my father, who was the master marketer of all—he truly sold ice to Eskimos! And to my mother, who marketed grace by example. My family has always been encouraging and supportive.

To my many colleagues in the Association of Business Simulation and Experimental Learning Association, whose annual meetings have been a constant source of help and inspiration.

Jerald R. Smith

To my family for their encouragement and support. To several colleagues— Peter Mears, Dick Herden, Lyle Sussman, Bruce Kemelgor, and Mike Carrell—for their inspiration and counsel.

Peggy A. Golden

We would both like to acknowledge the support and leadership of Robert Taylor, Dean of the School of Business, University of Louisville. And cheers to staff members of the school—Jane Goldstein, Jan Pollard, Denise Nance, and Laura Ahrens—for their excellent services.

Finally, without the helpful suggestions of professors from many colleges and universities, this new and enhanced second edition would not have been possible. Among those who have offered outstanding ideas are the following:

Kenneth Goodenday

Robert Atkins

Doug Strope

Eric Panitz

Ted Erickson

Jean Shaneyfelt

Alan Flaschner

Mark Green

Carmelita Troy

Dick Shaw

Phil Noll

John Page

Rich Beacherer

Frank Calabretta

Larry Estepp

MARKETER: A Simulation
Second Edition

1

AN OVERVIEW OF MARKETING AND SIMULATION

INTRODUCTION TO SIMULATION

Welcome to the exciting world of simulation! A simulation provides a unique opportunity for the student to practice managing an organization on a continuous basis — to make decisions, to see how they work out, and, if necessary, to try again! Thus, students get "hands on" experience manipulating key marketing variables in a dynamic setting.

Simulation techniques have been used for some time in attempts to create marketing models that can explain certain results. In this simulation, we have combined real-world marketing reactions with a marketing environment found in this type of competitive situation. This model takes the decisions each team makes and simulates consumers' reactions. The relative *appropriateness* of each team's decisions is reported on the team's marketing division report.

Managers must make decisions based on imperfect information, great uncertainties, and time constraints, and so this simulation reflects these factors. You will need to get as much information as possible through the market research reports provided, to keep good records in order to study the interactions between the marketing variables, then to make your decisions (without looking back!). The next step is to study and analyze the printout provided each team, then to polish up your decisions for the next round. We recommend that you do not use the "stab in the dark" method of making decisions but rather plan to hold certain variables constant while you manipulate other variables. This will help you to determine which marketing mix variables are more effective in generating sales. (Note: Do NOT rely on information gathered from others who have competed in the simulation. The instructor can change the competitive environment of the simulation for each class!)

Each company in this simulation is composed of one to five class members who assume responsibility for the operation of their assigned firm. The method of organizing your team normally is left up to each team by the instructor. Your company is competing with other teams (up to 20 total) in the home entertainment center industry. Teams are expected to establish objectives, plan their strategy, then make the required marketing decisions dictated by these plans. Decisions are turned in to the instructor on appropriate forms. These decisions are inputted into the computer, which analyzes them and prepares a report for each team concerning its sales and profits. This is done for several iterations.

All teams make a few mistakes throughout the simulation, so they tend to equal out. Keep your spirits up — and good luck!

OVERVIEW OF THE MARKETING PROCESS

What Is Marketing?

Marketing, like other disciplines, may be defined in several ways. Some popular definitions describe it as the performance, processes, and systems that lead organizations to produce goods and services to meet the needs of a clientele. The definition we use is considerably broader in scope and can easily be put into operation:

Marketing consists of individual and organizational activities that facilitate and expedite exchange relationships in a dynamic environment through the creation, distribution, promotion, and pricing of goods, services, and ideas.[1]

The model allows us to define a set of variables that can be integrated into the organization's activities. These variables are shown in Figure 1.1 as the "four Ps" of the marketing mix. The environment is a set of forces that affects the organization but are out of its control. The consumer (buyer) is the dependent variable here, seeking the benefits provided by the organization's goods or services.

FIGURE 1.1 THE DYNAMIC MARKETING ENVIRONMENT

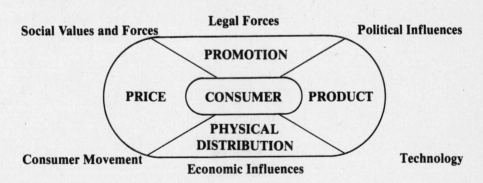

[1] William M. Pride and O. C. Ferrell, *Marketing: Basic Concepts and Decisions,* 5th ed. (Boston: Houghton Mifflin Company, 1987), p. 7.

Influencing Buying Behavior

There are many influences on consumer buying behavior. Some of these can be controlled by the marketer and some are inalterable characteristics of the customer. These influences can be sorted into four major groups associated with the buyer, the seller, the product, and the situation.

The buyer and the situation are largely out of the marketer's control. The buyer comes to the exchange relationship with cultural, social, psychological, and personal or demographic characteristics that are already established. The situation surrounding the purchase can be affected by time pressures, chance encounters with friends, adverse weather, or an unfavorable economic climate. Product and seller influences are more easily controlled by the organization. The marketer can design product attributes to appeal to the target buyer. The seller can create a marketplace image that will help the buyer form an opinion about the firm or the product. Figure 1.2 below shows the factors that influence buying behavior.

FIGURE 1.2 FACTORS THAT INFLUENCE BUYING BEHAVIOR

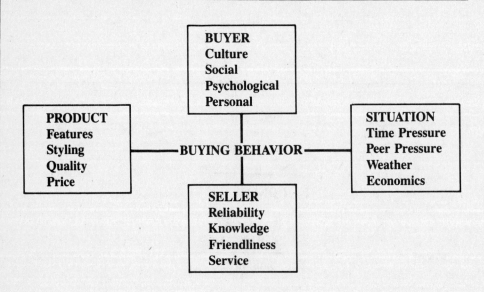

What are the major influences on consumer purchases of your product?

The concept of exchange is crucial to the definition used here. In an exchange relationship, four conditions must exist:

- There must be two or more individuals or groups participating.
- Each must have something of value wanted by the other.
- Each must be willing to give up something of value to gain what the other party has.
- The parties must have a mechanism to communicate with each other.

A good marketing plan begins with identification of the benefits sought by the other party. The idea is to build a product that meets a need rather than to build a product and then try to sell it to the public. A commonly used example is the railroads, which would not have lost their financial viability if they had been more sensitive to meeting the need for transporting goods and people by whatever method possible rather than over two iron rails. The conscientious marketer must be knowledgeable about the "package of benefits" that the consumer is seeking in the purchase of a good or service. This "set" is the value that is brought to the exchange relationship. All activities that are developed to implement the marketing variables should be guided by the package of benefits sought.

Determining Marketing Strategies

In order to begin the process of selecting activities to implement the marketing variables, it is necessary to develop a marketing plan for a product or service. There are many methods for doing this, but all have these certain elements in common:

1. *Define the business.* It is necessary to develop a written definition in terms of what benefits are provided to whom through what medium. This should lead to overall organizational marketing goals.
2. *Analyze opportunities and threats.* Competition, organizational resources, and investment requirements must be reviewed carefully to determine whether each forms an opportunity for growth or poses a potential threat to the organization. Some elements represent both opportunities and threats. A competitor may pose a threat while at the same time creating a favorable environment for your product or service in the marketplace through extensive generic advertising.
3. *Establish marketing objectives.* Organizational goals and opportunity and threat analysis permit the establishment of marketing objectives that should fit the organization and the product or service. Marketing

objectives usually set volume and market penetration levels and a time-frame for their achievement.

4. *Select target markets and a marketing mix.* This is the implementation phase of a strategic market plan and is frequently the result of extensive marketing and product research.

5. *Establish standards for evaluating results.* A strategic plan for any organizational function should be evaluated for successes and failures. This means that a marketing plan must have some quantifiable measures of its accomplishment. Volume increases, market share, and contribution to profits are some measures used to evaluate marketing strategies.

The section that begins on page 32 in Chapter 2 can help your team establish a strategic market plan.

Outsourcing Production

To contain production costs, many American firms are negotiating with foreign producers to produce their products for them. Although companies have contracted some production for years, these new "hollow corporations" have abandoned the production process entirely, choosing instead to create joint ventures with companies in industrialized foreign countries that are able to produce goods at a lower unit cost. This strategy, known as *outsourcing,* allows the organization to concentrate its efforts and expertise on marketing while delegating manufacturing problems to a separate company.

Outsourcing is invisible to the consumer, who may believe that he or she is buying a well-known American brand. The prices of the goods may be lower than products manufactured in the United States due to manufacturing efficiencies and the tariff protections that apply to certain imported goods. Although the quality of these products does not appear to be affected, business futurists are concerned that the separation of production and marketing may create barriers to technological advancement and innovation by American firms.

What are the advantages of having a service firm that focuses on marketing? Based on the strategic market planning process, what problems or obstacles does this type of organization face?

Classification of the Product or Service

To aid in the planning process, most organizations try to classify their product or service along several dimensions. This is a useful process because it helps in defining the marketing variables and in selecting a market niche. Organizations have an additional interest in classifying new products. Most companies have a portfolio of products and services. Each product or service has a life cycle, and companies with several products may have a portfolio of products that are in different stages of the life cycle. (The life cycle of a product is a retrospective analysis of time and revenues.) There are four stages in a product's life cycle: introduction, growth, maturity, and decline. The ideal product portfolio has a combination of products at various stages in the life cycle. Each stage requires a different set of marketing strategies. Figure 1.3 shows a typical product life cycle graph. Classification of products on this model assists marketers in establishing realistic objectives and strategies.

FIGURE 1.3 PRODUCT LIFE CYCLE

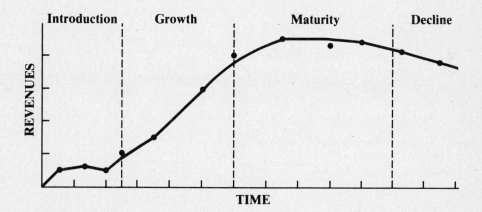

2

THE ENVIRONMENT
AND PROCESS

THE INDUSTRY

The company your team is operating is one of several in the home entertainment industry. Although this is not a new segment of the consumer electronics business, recent technological advances have created new products, and many companies are moving into this niche. Most of the products have had slow initial consumer adoption, with growth beginning two to three quarters after introduction.

The typical configuration of competing equipment is a receiver with electronic tuning, two three-way speakers, a dubbing tape deck, and a turntable. There are some additional peripheral devices that can be added if the consumer wants. This type of equipment often is distributed through wholesalers who make direct sales to retailers. The product reaches the ultimate consumer through specialty stores, department stores, and off-price merchandisers. There is some evidence that discount mail-order houses also are offering this type of product.

Your competition is a moderately priced, complete stereo sound system for home use (see Figure 2.1). A survey of the industry reveals that typical manufacturing costs are in the $350 range and that the wholesale price has stayed close to $500. The complete set retails at between $650 and $1,000. Of course, there are more expensive configurations and less expensive compact stereos, but these generally are targeted at other market segments and are not your competition.

PRODUCT DEMAND

Total market potential for this product is affected by forces in the marketing environment, including economic conditions, technological advancements, price, research and development (R & D) expenditures (to improve the product and provide quality control), other factors in the marketing mix, and some unknown variables that affect consumer adoption behavior. The environment is somewhat turbulent and can change rapidly. Teams are encouraged to purchase Market Research Study 1 (or 2), which gives an estimate of demand for the next quarter (or four quarters). This estimate combines the overall condition of the economy and current consumer demand for the product. The data are given in the form of an index number — a "business index" — and are based on a starting point of 100. An estimate of 105 indicates that demand is expected to go up 5 percent in that quarter.

THE COMPANY

The company that your management team is operating is a recently formed division of a well-established electronics firm. It has been in operation for three quarters and the start-up team has been moved to another new venture. The sound system you are marketing contains an electronically tuned receiver, a dubbing tape deck, a turntable, two speakers, and a glass and wood cabinet. It is being manufactured to your specifications in Japan and sold under your company's brand name.

The start-up team has been purchasing the system for $350 and selling it to retailers in the present quarter for $500. The retailers have been selling the product to consumers at prices ranging from $699 to $999, in a "whatever the market will bear" policy. Selected past operating information is shown

FIGURE 2.1 YOUR HOME ENTERTAINMENT PRODUCT

in Figure 2.2. By charting some of these historic data, your team can begin to identify trends that should help in developing useful strategies for marketing decisions.

OBJECTIVES OF THE SIMULATION

A key objective of the simulation is to optimize the contribution of profits of this division toward corporate earnings. We should note that although profits in the short term should not be underemphasized, your marketing team may choose to forgo some short-term profits while building the division for future higher payoffs. (However, don't forget the simulation does have a specified period of time to run.) Teams should not manage the firm for the short term only and "end play" the simulation to maximize profits at the end of play. This would not be operating the division in the best interest of the parent firm amd the stockholders. In other words, at the end of the simulation, the parent firm (your instructor) will be expecting to evaluate a "healthy, going concern." Other important objectives that the instructor (or teams) may want to establish include

1. implementation of marketing strategies that capture a maximum (or optimum) market share.
2. management of operations in a cost-effective manner.
3. observation of good business ethics and standards that will increase the value of corporate goodwill.
4. maintenance of reasonable inventories.
5. knowledge of certain marketing mix relationships through experimentation and good market research practices.

THE DECISION-MAKING PROCESS

Marketing Management

Pricing

The pricing variable cannot be described simply as an activity. The price of a good or service frequently affects consumer demand. If there is a strong

FIGURE 2.2 PAST OPERATING DATA

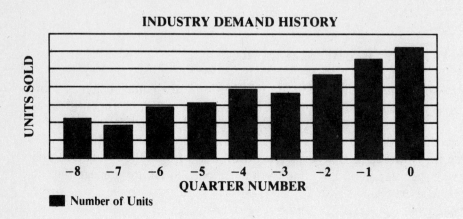

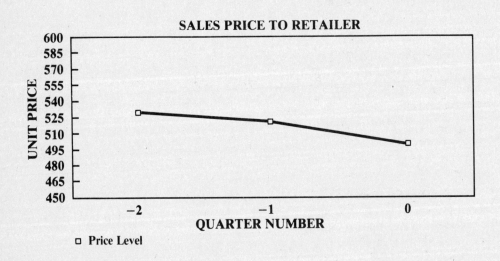

FIGURE 2.2 PAST OPERATING DATA (Continued)

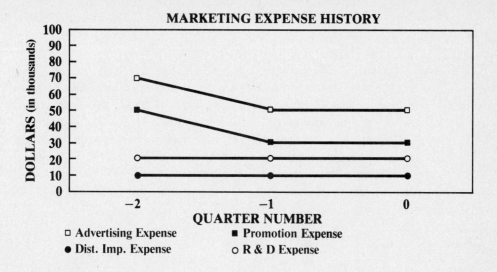

MARKETING EXPENSE HISTORY

□ Advertising Expense   ■ Promotion Expense
● Dist. Imp. Expense   ○ R & D Expense

Packaging

Q. When is a carton not a carton?
A. When it is the display for a consumer good.

Packaging is sometimes called the fifth P in the marketing mix. Many companies spend a significant portion of their marketing budget in developing a container that will protect the product, be easy to handle, and have visual appeal. Market research firms have determined that certain colors have greater appeal than others and that some products should be displayed (in clear plastic "bubble packaging," for example) while others are best concealed in an attractive wrapper.

Small home appliances and consumer electronics traditionally have been shipped in sturdy corrugated boxes that have more utility than eye appeal. This was due to the fact that retailers displayed just samples of products on showroom floors and kept their stock in separate locations. The recent influx of discounters, self-service and warehouse-type retailers have forced manufacturers to reconsider the packaging of these "big-ticket" items. One personal computer manufacturer shipped its merchandise in attractive white and pastel boxes that can be stacked on showroom floors.

Create a mock-up of a packaging design for your product.

negative relationship between price and demand, the demand is *elastic*. If price has no effect on demand, the demand is *inelastic*. Marketing theorists feel that pricing strategies can help to *pull* a product into the marketplace when demand is elastic.

Your sound system has been priced to retailers in the latest period for $500, and they in turn have been selling to the final consumer in the $699 to $999 range. The introductory price two periods earlier was $530; last period it was $520. Typically, in the early stages of a product's life cycle, prices are higher as firms attempt to "skim" the market. Later, as more competition appears and the supply of new competing products increases, prices usually decline. It is too soon to gauge the impact of price on sales, but there does appear to be an increase in the number of competitors and discount outlets.

Advertising

The advertising variable can be implemented through a variety of activities that have various effects on consumer behavior. Advertising strategies are designed to affect consumer buying behavior and often are referred to as *pulling* strategies. There are many methods for advertising a product or service. Each has a different amount of reach or effect on consumer decisions. Advertising usually is priced according to the reach of the medium employed. Your firm has maintained a large portion of its marketing mix in advertising, spending $70,000 in the first quarter of operation and $50,000 in both the second and third quarters.

Sales Promotion

Sales promotion frequently is the marketing activity used to *push* the product through the channels of distribution into the marketplace. Typical sales promotion activities include the development of point-of-sale displays, and coupons, rebates, and other financial incentives to purchase a product. Sales promotion strategies often are utilized in short bursts to introduce a new product, to stimulate a slow-moving product, or to reduce inventories in a slow economy.

Sales promotion activities are rather costly. Your firm spent $30,000 on those activities in the first quarter of operation, increased it to $50,000 during the second quarter (mainly on in-store display materials), and cut back to $30,000 in the latest quarter.

Channel Efficiency

Choosing the best channel of distribution is one of the most difficult decisions facing a manufacturer or marketing organization. There are many direct and indirect costs that affect this variable and a large number of options. Some channels include distributors, wholesalers, manufacturers' agents, and direct sales. Channels should be selected for their effectiveness

Intermediary Levels in the Channel of Distribution

Intermediaries are individuals or organizations in the distribution channel that link the producer and the retailer. A direct channel has no intermediaries; other channels have one or more intermediaries. Occasionally, an intermediary acts as both distributor and retailer. The type of distribution channel an organization chooses helps determine its promotional strategies — and whether those strategies are aimed at distributors, retailers, or both.

Each step in the distribution channel takes the product closer to the retailer. As a distribution channel grows longer, the costs of bringing a product from producer to retailer increase and the producer's control of that channel decreases. However, the use of intermediaries can increase the number of potential customers (e.g., retailers) for the manufacturer's product.

The firm operated by your team is using a medium-length channel structure, like the one shown here in Figure 2.3:

FIGURE 2.3 DISTRIBUTION CHANNELS

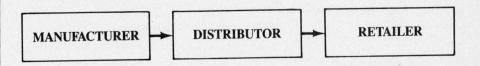

Can you design a channel improvement that would expedite the movement of your product? Develop an advertising and sales promotion plan that reaches the necessary entities in your distribution channel.

and their efficiency. The length of a channel (i.e., the number of organizations in the channel) is affected by the nature of the retailer, the classification of the product, and the consumer buying behavior associated with the product.

Home sound systems are sold in a wide variety of outlets. Your firm has spent $10,000 each quarter during its first three quarters of operation on distribution improvement. Expenditures for distribution improvement are used to improve the cost efficiency of delivering the product to the retailer. Some of these methods include operating one's own truck fleet, selling to wholesalers who take title to the goods, and joining producer/owner/distributor cooperatives. One can determine channel efficiencies by calculating a breakeven point for selling costs per channel against dollars of sales.

Channels of distribution are prone to develop conflict, which can be costly to the producer and the retailer. This conflict occurs when the goals and objectives of the various elements (organizations) in the channel are not in alignment. An example would be the failure of a wholesaler to deliver a product to a retailer in a timely fashion. The retailer blames the manufacturer for the inefficiency. Distribution improvement expenses sometimes are allocated toward resolving this kind of conflict and improving efficiency as well as effectiveness in the distribution channel.

Research and Development

Product research serves two purposes: It provides the quality control and customer service dimension usually associated with a high-quality product; and it allows the firm to make technological advancements and improvements in the product. Research activities usually are aimed at responding to environmental forces such as technological advances and social issues. Less frequently, R & D activities are implemented to satisfy government regulatory mandates. The electronics industry is characterized by a turbulent environment and has felt pressure from many environmental factors to maintain a high level of research and product improvement activities.

Although your firm does not manufacture the product you are selling, you are providing the Japanese manufacturer with all of the technical specifications to manufacture the product specifically for the American marketplace. Your R & D department also provides suggestions and actual methods for changing the product to keep up with your competition. Your firm spent $20,000 during each of the last three quarters to improve the product and keep pace with competitors.

Sales Force

The sales force sometimes is included in the promotion variable, although it can be viewed as the mortar for the other variables. There are several strategies for maintaining a sales force, and all have different costs and benefits. The two most commonly used are (1) sales personnel employed and supervised directly by the company and (2) independent sales agents such as manufacturers' representatives or jobbers. The in-house sales force is more expensive to the company but is well suited to sell a product or service that needs technical support. Independent sales agents frequently carry several related products, have wide distribution networks, and are paid on commission; but they provide less technical support. The type of sales force the

---

Developing New Products

New-product development is a costly time-consuming effort. Much like the problem-solving process, it begins with idea generation, then moves through alternative selection, development and testing, implementation through marketing and business strategies, and commercialization. New products may be the result of consumer needs or the result of creative research and development activities. Many products take two or three years and large amounts of development dollars to travel from idea to commercialization, and commercialization does not guarantee market adoption. The costs of this development — sunk costs — are borne by the company.

Examples of heavy investments in new products that had high payoffs include Apple's MacIntosh computer, Bausch and Lomb's hydrophyllic plastic (soft contact lenses), and Sony's videocassette recorder.

One technique used to generate ideas is brainstorming. Participants create a list of ideas without commenting on the quality of those ideas at the time they are articulated. Then, the list is refined until a reasonable new product (or service) emerges that is consistent with the business of the firm.

Use the brainstorming technique to generate a new product (or service) for your company.

---

organization selects is a function of the product's stage in the product life cycle, the type of product, and the need to implement push versus pull strategies.

Your company employs and trains its own sales force in order to provide good technical support and customer service. A certain level of sales staff is needed regardless of sales volume; this can be considered a fixed cost. However, certain push strategies increase the number of salespersons needed. The additional unit sales generated are a direct reflection of manipulating this variable; this cost, then, could be viewed as a variable cost of sales.

Your divisional marketing report includes sales personnel as an overhead expense because their salaries could be charged off to more than one product if you were operating with the two-product option. Each salesperson spends three months (one quarter) in training before being sent into the field. All sales personnel are paid $8,000 per quarter, starting with the training period. Your team also has the option of paying the sales force a commission or bonus on sales. This is inputted as x dollars paid per unit sold. (Note: It is important to keep this item in even dollar amounts so there are no decimals needed on the decision form.)

Operations Management

Goods Ordered and Accepted

In any manufacturing industry, there is a certain level of shrinkage of the product in inventory. This is also true with a product made to specifications, like your firm's sound system. Goods that are damaged in transit also are included as shrinkage; in addition, a specific shipment or portion thereof may get lost in transit or be shipped to a wrong location. All products must be checked before they are accepted from the manufacturing firm, and damaged or nonworking goods should be returned. This protects your quality control to your customers, contains unnecessary expenses, and notifies your supplier of its errors.

Shrinkage is often measured as a specific percentage of total product. In your firm, shrinkage has been running at about 5.4 percent during the two previous quarters of operation (e.g., 4,254 units received and usable ÷ 4,500 units ordered = 94.5% delivered and 5.4% not delivered). It is crucial to keep track of shrinkage because it affects the total inventory available for sale.

Cost of Goods

The manufacturer offers quantity discounts for your purchases of the home entertainment units per the following schedule:

Units	Cost per Unit
0 – 2,499	$400
2,500 – 3,999	375
4,000 – 6,999	350
7,000 – 8,999	342
9,000 and up	338

Inventory Management

Management of inventory is a difficult component of operations for many companies. A firm needs to have sufficient product to meet anticipated demand during any operating period; at the same time, it should not have too much capital invested in excessive inventory. In other words, there is an optimum inventory level. There are various mathematical models and methods used to calculate the optimum level of inventory, among them the economic order quantity (EOQ). Forecasts often are used to calculate desired inventory levels, but this method is only as good as the forecasts. All forecasts have some margin of error in them. Not having enough inventory to meet demand (termed a *stockout*) causes customers to look for other suppliers, while excess inventory can be a burdensome cost to the company.

Your firm uses a weighted average accounting system for inventory valuation. This means that the cost of the product for accounting purposes is calculated at the average cost of all units in inventory. The fixed cost of maintaining your firm's warehousing operation is $9,000 per quarter. This is the normal cost of receiving and shipping the usual volume of products each quarter. In addition, it currently costs $20 per unit for each unsold unit each quarter in extra storage costs to carry over unsold inventory (this is based on the number of units in ending inventory each period).

Financial Management

Contribution Margin of the Product

Marketing expenses, which include advertising, sales promotion, distribution improvements, and product research and development, are expenses that can be varied as the strategies for marketing the sound system are changed. Because these expenses are controlled directly by your division's marketing team, close supervision of these costs and their relative effectiveness is mandatory. The parent company will be judging your marketing management effectiveness, in large part, on the "bottom line" (profit) contribution of your division. The following section shows how this figure is calculated:

Revenues: 4,077 units sold × unit selling price $500 =		$2,038,500
Less cost of goods sold: 4,077 units × unit cost $350 =		1,426,950
Gross margin (revenues less cost)		$ 611,550

Less expenses:

Advertising	$50,000
Sales promotion	30,000
Distribution imprv.	10,000
Bonus paid on sales	0
R & D	20,000

Subtract total expenses	110,000
Contribution toward fixed costs	$ 501,550

If your marketing strategies are efficient as well as effective, compared to the rest of the industry, your contribution toward your fixed expenses will be higher than your competitors' and your bottom line (profits) should be higher.

Other Fixed and Overhead Costs

Some elements of overhead costs are under the control of the marketing team, while others (e.g., administrative costs) are established automatically for you according to sales volume. Areas in which you have some discretion include the number of salespeople in training and in the field, inventory levels and related expenses, market research expenses, and other incidental expenses that you may incur from time to time. An overhead cost that you have little control over is administrative cost. Administrative cost is computed on the following schedule:

Sales (in units)	Fixed Cost (per quarter)
0 − 5,000	$200,000
5,001 − 6,000	220,000
6,001 − 7,000	240,000
7,001 − 8,000	260,000
8,001 − 9,000	280,000
Over 9,000	300,000

Total overhead expenses are deducted from the *contribution margin* of the product(s) to provide the *net contribution* of your division toward the parent firm's corporate overhead. The parent company has agreed to protect your division from financial distress in case of net losses during any quarter. However, your firm will be ranked against your competitors and downgraded if your performance results in a financial imposition on the parent company. It should be pointed out that net contribution should not be considered net profit because the parent company is covering certain nonallocated costs (e.g., cost of capital, income taxes, parent company overhead, etc.).

Marketing Research

Most successful marketing strategies include a viable market research program. Research activities may be carried out by an in-house group or by firms that specialize in marketing research. Through the process of field research, companies are able to determine many aspects of consumer buying behavior that affect marketing strategies. Among market research activities are focus groups to determine consumer benefits sought, surveys to determine the demographic characteristics of potential customers, and follow-up studies to determine adoption behaviors. Because of the turbulent environment in which the home entertainment industry operates, your firm undoubtedly will benefit from selecting certain types of market research information available to you. Generally, any information your firm purchases is valid only during the next quarter. On the next page is a list of the available studies and their costs.

MARKET RESEARCH STUDIES AND ASSOCIATED COSTS

		Cost
1.	Estimate of demand for the next quarter	$2,000
2.	Estimate of demand for the next four quarters	9,000
3.	Number of salespersons for each firm last quarter	4,000
4.	Estimate of average industry sales this period	5,000
5.	Wholesale price each firm is charging its retailers	5,000
6.	Estimate of average advertising this period	5,000
7.	Estimate of average sales promotion this period	5,000
8.	Estimate of average R & D expenditure this period	5,000

Note: The cost of the various research studies you order will be charged to your firm automatically in the Marketing Research Expense category.

Second-product Option

Note: This feature of the simulation is optional and can be used only at the discretion of your instructor.

Recent studies of component sound system owners reveal that customers similar to yours are interested in purchasing equalizers and compact disc players. A reputable distributor will sell you a compact disc player that is compatible with your product and other sound systems in your industry for $40 to $50 each. There is no specific sales history information available on this equipment because your firm has never handled it before. Information from the industry on similar products indicates that the markup to the retailer appears to be between 30 and 150 percent.[1]

Your sales force can sell the package to the same retailers who currently carry your sound system. Although the addition of this package would be a positive selling point for your product and a source of additional income, providing customer service information would place an added burden on your division, the home office staff, and field sales personnel.

Your cost for the compact disc player set is as follows: less than 5,000 units, $50 each; 5,000 and over, $40 each. The inventory cost is not as high as it is for Product 1 because the package is physically smaller. Your warehouse manager feels she can handle the product with little additional cost (esti-

[1]One expert in the field has estimated that the demand for a compact disc player package would be about 50 percent of a firm's sound system sales (in units).

mated at $4 per unit of ending inventory). However, there is a possibility that new technology may improve compact disc players, making those in inventory obsolete (or at best, you would have to dispose of them at greatly reduced prices).

Competitive Marketing Intelligence Systems

The use of computers for marketing activities has grown exponentially in the past decade. Initially, computers provided, among other things, on-line data bases that allowed marketing and sales managers to search for and sort customers' files in order to determine sales trends. As personal computers grew smaller and more portable, sales personnel became able to communicate with the corporate marketing data base while they were in the field by using conventional telephone lines.

Today, marketing managers have a new tool: computerized competitive marketing intelligence systems. These systems permit the analysis of marketing problems using information about the environment as well as internal historical data and economic trend analysis. The systems consist of three parts: expert software that has the ability to learn new rules as it functions; access to large data bases, among them PIMS (Profit Impact on Marketing Strategy); and the internal data of the corporation. Users do not have to be computer experts because these systems are able to process common English inquiries.

Some of the activities that can be performed on these intelligence systems include comparisons of the company to the marketplace, projections about market penetration and profitability under various scenarios (e.g., the best-possible case, the most likely case, and so on), and futuristic glimpses of customer and competitor behavior. Competitive marketing intelligence systems are still very expensive and require main-frame computers capable of processing large sets of data. However, they appear to be following the downward trend of information costs and should be available to small companies by the end of the decade.

In what ways would your firm benefit from a competitive marketing intelligence system?

Analysis of Printout for Quarter 0

Figure 2.4 shows a sample computer printout for the most recent period (Period 0). The printout indicates the condition of the firm you are taking over. In order to better understand the information on it, locate the items that are discussed below on the figure.

Profit and Loss Analysis

The top portion of the printout lists the division's sales of Product 1 (4,077 units), the current selling price ($500), and gross revenues ($2,038,500 = 4,077 X $500). Cost of goods sold is your cost of those units sold ($350) times the number of units sold (4,077 units). The gross margin, also known as the gross profit margin, is the difference between gross sales revenues and the cost of goods sold ($611,550).

Advertising ($50,000), sales promotion ($30,000), distribution improvements ($10,000), R & D ($20,000), and sales bonus expenses are listed according to the decisions made by the marketing team; their amounts are completely within your control. The total sales expense ($110,000) is subtracted from the gross margin to show the contribution of the product ($501,550) as a result of marketing strategies.

Sales force expenses are calculated at the rate of $8,000 per person (5 persons @ $8,000 = $40,000), including those who may be in training. Inventory expense includes a fixed $9,000 plus $20 per unit times the ending inventory shown at the bottom of the report [$9,000 + ($20 X 365) = $16,300]. Market research information is shown as a total of all packages of information purchased ($2,000); and administrative expense is fixed according to the volume of sales ($200,000). Although your decisions do have an impact on the level of this expense, the simulation will calculate the dollar amounts for you. The overhead costs of these decisions ($258,300) is subtracted from the contribution of Product 1 to yield the net contribution of your division toward corporate overhead ($243,250).

Total Asset Valuation

The total assets allocated to your marketing division are calculated and printed out near the center of the page. This figure allows you to determine the return on assets ratio each period. This important financial ratio allows firms of different sizes to compare their relative financial success. Form 5 is included in Chapter 8 to help you make various financial ratio calculations.

FIGURE 2.4   SAMPLE PRINTOUT OF QUARTER 0

COMPANY 1 MARKETING DIVISION QUARTERLY REPORT   PERIOD 0
INDUSTRY A

```
SALES-PRODUCT 1:  4077 UNITS @ 500            $2038500
                  COST OF GOODS SOLD @ 350    1426950
                  GROSS MARGIN....................... $611550

EXPENSES FOR PRODUCT 1:
                  ADVERTISING              $ 50000
                  SALES PROMOTION            30000
                  DISTRIBUTION IMPRV.        10000
                  BONUS PAID ON SALES            0
                  RESEARCH & DEVELOPMENT     20000
                    TOTAL SALES EXPENSE............. $110000
                      CONTRIBUTION OF PRODUCT 1............. $501550

OVERHEAD EXPENSES:
                  SALES FORCE – 5 IN FIELD  $ 40000
                  SALES FORCE – 0 TRAINING       0
                  INVENTORY EXPENSE          16300
                  MARKETING RESEARCH          2000
                  ADMINISTRATIVE EXPENSE    200000
                  OTHER EXPENSES                 0

                  TOTAL OVERHEAD EXPENSES ................ $258300

                  NET CONTRIBUTION TO CORP. OVERHEAD............. $243250


              ** ASSETS OF THIS DIVISION THIS PERIOD $931600 **


                      *** INVENTORY ANALYSIS ***
```

	PRODUCTS ORDERED	PRODUCTS RECEIVED	BEGINNING INVENTORY	AVAILABLE FOR SALE	LESS SALES	ENDING INVENTORY	EST. OF LOST SALES
PRODUCT 1:	4500	4257	185	4442	4077	365	0
PRODUCT 2:	0	0	0	0	0	0	0

*** MARKET RESEARCH ***

BUSINESS INDEX FORECAST FOR NEXT PERIOD IS 101

*** NEWS MESSAGES ***

TEAMS NEED TO BE VERY CAREFUL IN ADDING THEIR VERIFICATION TOTAL. SOMETHING
VERY UNPLEASANT COULD HAPPEN.... GOOD LUCK TO ALL TEAMS!

Industry Demand

The total number of units sold in Period 0 is equal to 4,077 units times the total number of companies (teams). Future total industry demand (in units) can be forecasted by applying the business index to current total sales. (Hint: You must buy Market Research Study 4, an estimate of average industry sales this period.) Example: Average industry sales (4,500) times the business index (1.05) times the number of companies competing (10) equals 47,250 units.

Inventory Analysis

The next section of the printout consists of an inventory analysis. Products ordered are the units that were ordered by your company (4,500 units). Products received and accepted are those units that arrived and were found to be in usable condition (4,254 units). Beginning inventory (189) is added to goods received and accepted to determine all goods available for sale (4,442). Sales for this quarter (4,077 units) are subtracted to calculate ending inventory (365 units).

Inventory carrying charges, which are listed under the overhead expenses, are calculated on these remaining units. An estimate of lost sales for this period (0) is based on the sales manager's calculation of losses due to lack of sufficient inventory. This may be caused by inadequate ordering or excessive shrinkage.

Market Research Information

The market research information purchased by you is printed near the bottom of the printout. The cost of the various studies is charged automatically to you as part of overhead expenses.

Industry News Message

In this section is pertinent information concerning your industry or instructional information from the game administrator. If the incident version of the simulation is being used, relevant information concerning your incident decision(s) will be printed in the lower portion of the printout. Information concerning an incident could be received immediately or several periods after its occurrence.

Second-product Option

If you are marketing a second product, the sales revenue and expense analysis will appear immediately below that of Product 1, and the expenses will be subtracted from the revenues to calculate a contribution of Product 2. Because the second product can be sold through the same sales force, the same overhead analysis will apply to both products. However, the costs are likely to be somewhat higher due to the expenses incurred with larger amounts of inventory and sales.

PREPARING THE DECISION FORM

After your team has decided what its strategy will be for the following quarter, a decision form should be completed and turned in to your instructor. A copy of this form for the previous quarter is shown in Figure 2.5. Refer to it as you read this section.

Some general rules:

1. Write legibly with a dark pencil or pen (not with a #3 or #4 pencil!).
2. Use your best printing style because the person who inputs your decisions on the computer does not have time to call each team about questionable entries. Examples: Zeros that are not quite closed on top look like sixes; sevens with a small top look like ones; threes and fives can be confused.
3. Do not use decimals anywhere on the form. At the wholesale level, odd-dollar pricing ($499.95 or $99.50) makes little difference in sales over the nearest dollar amount. Likewise, when inputting a bonus paid to salespersons for each unit sold, please use an even dollar amount (e.g., $1, $2, $3).
4. If you are not selling Product 2, leave all the boxes relating to that product *blank*. All other boxes should have a zero if you are not using them (see, for example, the unused market research lines in the figure). This is not a critical item, but it does help the person inputting the decision forms.
5. Once you have placed all your decisions on the form, add all items [from products ordered (item 1) through incident response (item 20)]. This is the verification total. It has nothing to do with the decisions, but it does give the person inputting the numbers a check on the input. If you put in an incorrect verification total, it really slows the process up. Don't be

FIGURE 2.5 EXAMPLE OF A DECISION FORM WITH PREVIOUS PERIOD'S DECISIONS

FORM 9: DECISION FORM

COMPANY NO. _1_ PERIOD NO. _0_

INDUSTRY _A_

PRODUCT 1:	1.	PRODUCTS ORDERED	4500
	2.	PRICE	$ 500
	3.	ADVERTISING	$ 50,000
	4.	SALES PROMOTION	$ 30,000
	5.	DISTRIBUTION IMPRV.	$ 10,000
	6.	BONUS PAID (per unit)	$ 0
	7.	R & D	$ 20,000
PRODUCT 2:	8.	PRODUCTS ORDERED	____
	9.	PRICE	$ ____
	10.	ADVERTISING	$ ____,000
	11.	SALES PROMOTION	$ ____,000
	12.	DISTRIBUTION IMPRV.	$ ____,000
	13.	BONUS PAID (per unit)	$ ____
	14.	R & D	$ ____,000
	15.	SALESPERSON CHANGE (+ or –)	0
	16.	MARKET RESEARCH #	1
	17.	MARKET RESEARCH #	0
	18.	MARKET RESEARCH #	0
	19.	MARKET RESEARCH #	0
	20.	INCIDENT RESPONSE #	0
		VERIFICATION TOTAL	5,111

Note: Use *whole numbers* only – do not use decimals anyplace. Add all the numbers that you have inserted from item 1 through item 20. Place total in the verification box (do not add the preprinted 000s). This is used to verify the correctness of the numbers as they are typed into the computer. This total *must* be correct or you will be fined. Place a zero in any blank not used but leave Product 2 blanks empty if you are not selling Product 2.

surprised if a tornado or some other catastrophe strikes your warehouse if this is not totalled correctly!

6. Remember, if you are discharging salespersons, use a minus sign in front of the number. Otherwise, the simulation assumes this is a positive number and hires salespersons and places them in training. It takes one quarter in training before a salesperson is given a territory and begins to generate sales.

7. Other notes from your instructor:

AIDS FOR TEAM ORGANIZATION AND DECISION MAKING

We recommend that each team prepare an organization chart depicting at least three levels in the organization. A team may organize itself in any manner it feels is best. Effective marketing can be planned and controlled by several types of organizations. The following are offered as some alternatives.

Production-centered Organization

Production management is central to this type of organization, which is reflected in the chart below. The advantages are good product innovation and tight cost controls. The disadvantages include greater distance from strategy planners to consumers, which makes it more difficult to respond and adapt to changes in the marketplace.

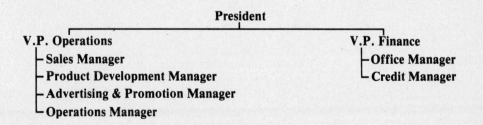

Sales-centered Organization

The philosophy behind this type of organization assumes that the central focus of the firm is the sales of the product or service. This type of organization has advantages for a mature product line in a company that has the capacity to produce as the marketplace demands. A disadvantage of sales-centered organization is the inability to respond to consumer changes or social forces that require product or production changes.

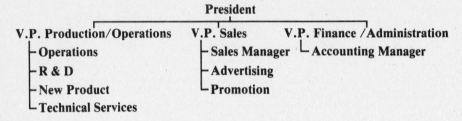

President

V.P. Production/Operations   V.P. Sales   V.P. Finance /Administration
- Operations   — Sales Manager   └ Accounting Manager
- R & D   — Advertising
- New Product   └ Promotion
- Technical Services

Franchising

A franchise is a contractual agreement between a manufacturer, distributor, or service organization (called the *franchisor*) and independent businesspeople (called *franchisees*). The difference between this arrangement and other contractual agreements is that the product (a good or service) is usually unique and may have been developed by the franchisor.

In a good franchise, both sides stand to profit. The franchisor gains a distribution organization with virtually no capital investment. This means that the network becomes profitable almost immediately. The franchisee gains a known product along with the technical expertise of the originator. In many cases, the franchisee gains exclusive rights to market the product or service in a geographic area. The costs of the agreement are contained in license fees, royalties, percentages of profits, or initial fees that are paid to the franchisor. Franchises are common in fast-food restaurants, automobile dealerships, and automobile service stations.

What are the benefits of a franchise organization for your product? What changes in your organization (e.g., new positions, changes in channels of distribution, and changes in advertising and sales promotion activities) might be necessary if you chose to franchise your product?

Market-centered Organization

The market-centered organization places the customer at the center of the organization. The advantage of this type of organization is its ability to respond rapidly to changes in consumer needs and technology. A disadvantage is that its distance from production concerns may inhibit actual product innovation.

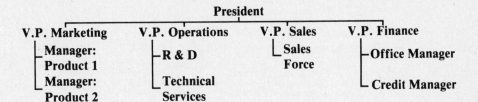

Segmented Versus Undifferentiated Products and Markets

Many companies choose to segment the market into discrete groups of consumers who exhibit different categories of product wants and needs. This division of the market permits the producer to "custom design" the elements in the marketing mix. Markets can be segmented along several lines: by socioeconomic or demographic characteristics (age, education, income), by geographic region (Midwest, South), and by consumers' expressed preferences for product attributes (sweeter, lighter). Of course, some producers choose to offer an undifferentiated product to the marketplace as a whole.

Market segmentation can create pockets of demand that may not generate as much profit for each product as could be generated by appealing to the marketplace as a whole with an undifferentiated product. On the other hand, it can be difficult to develop a marketing mix for an undifferentiated product. The final choice lies in the creativity and judgment of the marketing manager.

Is your market segmented or undifferentiated? How would you distinguish your product to a segmented market? To a mass market? Who do you think are the major purchasers of your product?

Choosing a Structure

On a one-person team, you do everything. A two-person team may want to have a financial or operations officer and a marketing officer. Three-person teams may want to divide into functional areas with chief executive, marketing, and operations officers. A four-person team could have a chief executive and one person to cover each of the major functional areas: finance, marketing, and operations. An alternative for a team with two products would be to assign the responsibility of each product to different individuals, or product managers (see the market-centered organization). When your team is considering the best method for organizing human and financial resources, you should debate such topics as corporate climate, product type and life cycle position, and desired distance from the marketplace.

ESTABLISHING PURPOSE, OBJECTIVES, AND PLANS

Purpose

The establishment of a purpose, or mission, for the division is the first step in the strategic planning process. This short statement answers several questions: What is our business? What is its value to our customers? Who are our customers? What will our business be? An effective mission statement is market oriented, feasible, motivating, and specific. It describes business domains in terms of product class, technology, customer group, market needs, or some combination of these. Contemporary marketing theorists believe that a market-centered definition of business is superior to a production or sales-centered definition.

A mission can be stated very simply; for example, "to market a complete home entertainment unit." Questions you should ask: Does this statement give continuity and new horizons to our business? Would the mission statement need changing for us to diversify or expand? Can our team develop a purpose or mission that allows for future flexibility but is not too broad?

Objectives

Objectives should specify commitments that are necessary to achieve the organization's purpose and the long-range goals of the organization's management. Objectives should give clear direction for accomplishment of the organization's purpose; they can serve to motivate those in the organization and can act as a control mechanism. A good objective specifies *what, by whom,* and *when.* Objectives should be measurable, quantifiable, and achievable.

Each team should establish its objectives as a firm. (Your instructor may want these objectives in written form.) Areas for which objectives could be established include the following:

1. Market standing
2. Sales level
3. Innovation/research and development
4. Profitability
5. Marketing mix
6. Social responsibility
7. Management development and training
8. Personnel relations

Plans

Merely establishing objectives, however, falls far short of completing the planning process for a division or company. The team must establish a plan of implementation to accomplish these objectives; these plans are called *tactical plans, strategic plans,* or *action plans.* For the purpose of this simulation, the action plan concept is used. This type of plan spells out in specific activities exactly how the organization's purpose and objectives are to be fulfilled. Form OB-1, which is included in Chapter 7, is a guide for helping the team establish its mission, objectives, and action plans.

Policy

After the team has established the general direction of the firm through the mission- and objective-setting processes, guidelines for daily activities must be prepared. These guidelines are called *policies*; they help with the integration of organizational goals by providing guidance yet allowing flexibility in decision making. Normally, policies are established so decisions do not have to be made concerning routine matters.

An example of a policy that would help the decision-making process in this simulation is one concerning advertising expenditures; for example, "the advertising budget will be determined by the previous quarter's sales." A range of acceptable limits may be established. A purchasing policy might be "to order the product at a level not to exceed 110 percent of estimated demand." Routine decisions are facilitated by establishing a method for accomplishing objectives before the fact; the development of policies, then, saves time during the actual decision-making process.

The following are some of the areas in which policies may be established:

1. Marketing budgets
2. Sales force level
3. Pricing
4. Inventory ordering
5. Technical and customer services
6. Market development
7. Innovations

Form P-1 (also in Chapter 7) can help your team develop a few key policies in important areas.

Company Log

In order to provide continuity among its decisions, each team may want to keep a log containing some or all of the following items:

1. Organization chart
2. Objectives
3. Strategies/action plans
4. Policies
5. Copies of each period's decision forms
6. Written notes explaining the rationale for each decision
7. Comparative charts, graphs, or tables containing the following information:
   a. Breakeven volume analysis
   b. Price-elasticity analysis
   c. Inventory management
   d. Pro forma income and expense statements
   e. Efficiency ratio analysis
   f. Unit cost
   g. Trend charts
   h. Market research analysis
   i. Profitability of the division

8. Copy of the quarterly printout
9. Copy of the justification of the incident decision
10. Any other information that could help you manage the division

Different types of forms and charts are included in this manual to help your team maintain the records needed for good decision making and control. Forms designed specifically to keep a log of quarterly decisions are included in Chapter 4.

Other Notes, Tips, and Tidbits

SELF-QUIZ

The objective of this quiz is to help you understand the important aspects of the simulation. After reading Chapter 2 twice, you should complete the quiz. You must have a full understanding of the mechanics of the simulation before you make your first decision.

1. Each decision period simulated by the program is equal to a

   _____ (month, quarter, year, various period).

2. What product(s) is your firm selling? _____

3. What price has your firm charged for its product in the most recent

   period? $ _____

4. What factors affect sales for a particular firm?

   a. _____   e. _____

   b. _____   f. _____

   c. _____   g. _____

   d. _____   h. _____

5. Inventory costs include a fixed $ _____ in warehouse expense

   each period plus $ _____ for each unit unsold at the end of
   each period.

6. The purpose of research and development is to (circle the correct items)

   a. create a product with more consumer appeal.
   b. create a higher-quality product.
   c. provide technical specifications for the manufacturer.
   d. create a more innovative product.

7. The budget for R & D last quarter was $ _____ .

8. The marketing mix for the firm includes (circle the appropriate items)

   a. price.   d. the number of salespersons.
   b. promotion.   e. sales force compensation.
   c. advertising.

9. The administrative expenses of the firm normally would include such items as officers' salaries, office rent and expenses, insurance, taxes,

   and utilities. The current cost of these expenses is $ _____ per quarter. These costs are on a sliding scale. The cost to maintain a sales

   level of 8,500 units per quarter is $ _____ .

10. There are currently _____ salespersons in the field, who are

    paid $ _____ per quarter each. The time required to train a new

    salesperson is _____ (none, two quarters, one quarter, four weeks).

11. The industrywide demand potential for Product 1 is affected by

    a. economic conditions.
    b. technological advancements.
    c. price.
    d. R & D expenditures.
    e. marketing mix effectiveness.
    f. consumer adoption behavior.

12. True or false: The gross margin shown on the printout represents the net profit per unit for the product.

13. True or false: The net contribution to corporate overhead shown on the printout could be equated to a firm's after-tax profit.

14. The current bonus paid to salespersons is $ _____ per unit.

15. True or false: The cost, if any, of decisions made on incidents is charged to each team automatically as Other Expenses.

16. True or false: A marketing audit should be accomplished by each firm whether it is required by the instructor or not.

17. Explain the purpose of the verification total on Form 9, the decision form.

    _____

    _____

18. True or false: Market Research Studies 1 and 2, estimates of demand for the next quarter and the next four quarters, consist only of an industry demand estimate.

Answers to the Self-Quiz

1. quarter (a three-month period)

2. Home entertainment center

3. $500

4. Price, advertising, sales promotion, distribution effectiveness, sales force effectiveness, R & D, overall product demand, other consumer and social environmental forces

5. $9,000; $20

6. All items are correct.

7. $20,000

8. All items are correct.

9. $200,000; $280,000

10. 5; $8,000; one quarter

11. a, b, c, d, f

12. False. It is total sales revenue less (only) the acquisition cost of those sales; it does not include any other expenses.

13. False. It does not include many expenses incurred by the parent company, among them income taxes and corporate overhead.

14. $0

15. True

16. True. The marketing audit provides a firm with a framework for a good self-analysis that should help keep it "on track." It should be done even if on a nonwritten, informal basis.

17. The verification total is used only to check the input of decision numbers for each team; it does not affect the firm's decisions. However, to keep the simulation administrator from re-adding your numbers, make sure the total is correct. See the bottom of the decision form for other important information.

18. False. The studies combine an estimate of overall consumer demand for the product with economic conditions. The business index is an index number with a starting value of 100.

3

DECISION INCIDENTS

This chapter contains twelve incidents, one for each decision period. The incidents are numbered to correlate with the decision periods. For example, Incident 1 is for Decision Period 1, Incident 2 is for Decision Period 2, and so on.

A class discussion point has been included at the end of each incident. This is a key topic that the class may want to discuss AFTER decisions are made.

INCIDENT 1

A survey published in a popular, nationally syndicated newspaper column indicates that most people use dubbing tape decks to copy prerecorded audio tapes. This practice, although hard to monitor, is a violation of copyright laws that results in losses to the developers of the original tape. Recently, there have been lawsuits filed against firms that manufacture equipment that has the potential of breaking the law (e.g., videocassette recorders, radar detectors).

Ironically, your advertising agency is just beginning an eight-week prime-time television blitz promoting the ability of your tape deck to reproduce tapes with the "low electronic noise of the original." The target audience is college students and young adults who are short on cash but are known buyers of sophisticated home audio equipment. Your advertising manager argues that the ads are not explicit about copying "proprietary" tapes; in addition, he believes that people will do it anyway.

Which of the following actions should you take?

1. Continue the ad campaign as planned and get informal feedback as to the positive and negative effects.
2. Continue the ad campaign as planned. Assign a staff member in your marketing department to research this topic and deliver a report within three months.
3. Quickly change the ad copy before the campaign begins to something that does not have ethical or legal implications. Overtime charges to revise the campaign are $12,000.
4. Continue the ad campaign as planned. Concurrently, have the business department at the local college conduct a review of the literature on the positive and negative effects of this type of advertising. The report will cost $3,000.
5. Cancel the ad campaign before it begins and find a different method for advertising your system. The cost of cancellation is $15,000.
6. Discontinue the planned campaign after four weeks and study the effect on sales and the audience. Cost: $6,000 to cancel the contract.

Enter your decision (1, 2, 3, 4, 5, or 6) on the decision form.

Class discussion point: Does a firm have a responsibility to abide by more than the "letter of the law"?

INCIDENT 2

Today's mail brought bad news. The deputy commissioner of the Federal Communications Commission has notified you that the power supply in some of your receivers has been causing reception problems in nearby televisions and telephones. The radio industry has experienced similar problems; some companies have responded by repairing the problem equipment and others have chosen to ignore it. At times, consumer advocacy groups have focused on interference with normal television reception, and the resulting bad publicity has affected sales in targeted companies.

Your technical service people in the R & D department estimate that repairing all of the receivers in transit and in stock will cost well over $100,000. But they believe that the problem does not affect every unit. How should your company proceed?

1. Ignore the warning until formal legal action is taken by the government.
2. Appoint a committee to study the problem and submit a report within nine months.
3. Fix the units in transit and in stock. This will cost $50,000, which will be charged to Other Expenses.
4. Test every fourth unit in stock and in transit, and repair only those that require it. This action would give you a better estimate of the magnitude of the problem but also would allow some imperfect units to be sold. The cost, $15,000, will be charged to Other Expenses.

Enter your decision (1, 2, 3, or 4) on the decision form.

Class discussion point: What responsibility does a firm have for the unintended, relatively harmless side effects of a product?

INCIDENT 3

The chairman of the board of the parent company has always had a high
level of community consciousness. When the board of directors met at your
facility last week, a suggestion was made that your team consider support-
ing some charitable or voluntary agencies. Although this will erode part of
your contribution toward corporate overhead, you are aware that efforts of
this nature can increase the reach or exposure of your organization. You are
considering several options:

a. Providing after-school classes and activities at no cost to middle- and
   high-school children in your area. Estimated costs: $5,000.
b. Participating in the loaned-executive program of the local United Fund
   agency and matching your employees' contributions. This will cost you
   $4,000 in matching grants plus the time of one of your junior executives
   for a two-month period ($3,000).
c. Sponsoring a program for insulating, repairing, and painting some of the
   substandard housing in the neighborhood of your sales facility. Cost:
   $10,000.
d. Joining a statewide coalition to promote educational literacy. Your contribution would assist in equipping and staffing the program, which is
   being operated by a nonprofit agency. Cost: $10,000.
e. Doing nothing until your organization's profitability warrants it.

(over)

Record on your decision form the decision number that corresponds to the item or items you want to implement. The cost shown is an annual cost that will be charged to Other Expenses in this quarter.

Decision Number to Record	Item(s) Above	Cost
1	a	$ 5,000
2	b	7,000
3	c	10,000
4	d	10,000
5	a, b	12,000
6	a, c or a, d	15,000
7	b, c or b, d	17,000
8	c, d	20,000
9	a, b, c or a, b, d	22,000
10	b, c, d	27,000
11	a, c, d	25,000
12	a, b, c, d	32,000
13	e	0

Class discussion point: Does a firm have a responsibility to a community beyond paying taxes and providing jobs? Who are the "stakeholders" in a firm? What is a firm's social responsibility?

INCIDENT 4

Market research and sales force reports point to large growth opportunities in the Canadian market. Your scan of the environment has led you to conclude that there are minimal cultural barriers and that consumer buying behavior is similar to that in the United States. Competition in Canada is about the same as it is in the United States as well. The demographic analysis shows a smaller wealthy population but a larger middle-income population in Canada, and the average age is about the same. Canadian politics are somewhat more socialistic, and distribution channels and outlets are regulated more closely. In addition, the exchange rate of Canadian and American dollars has experienced some fluctuations.

There are several important advantages of developing international markets: A Canadian operation will shelter you from U.S. government limits on exports and from excess tariffs; moreover, even limited market penetration could increase your sales substantially. The parent corporation says, "Do it on your own; our funds are tied up in other ventures!" However, it has agreed to forgive any contribution toward corporate overhead for two quarters. You estimate sales and profits may be meager for two years, but there is a good probability that the project will succeed after that.

Start-up costs will include additional expenses for marketing, for establishing a regional marketing office, for legal work, and for at least one extra salesperson. What should your team do?

1. Start up the Canadian operation immediately. The costs, $150,000, will be charged to Other Expenses as start-up costs divided equally over the next two quarters. You also need to hire at least one additional salesperson this period.
2. Study the situation for another year before making a decision.
3. Put the idea on the back burner indefinitely but not permanently.
4. Reject the idea completely so that all your time and effort can be devoted to making your domestic operation as successful as possible.

Enter your decision (1, 2, 3, or 4) on the decision form.

Class discussion point: What are the key considerations of entering a new market, especially a foreign market, for the first time?

INCIDENT 5

A large mail-order discounter in New York is accepting bids for 2,000 home entertainment stereo units. Although mail-order discounters have not been a particularly large segment of your business, your system appears to meet the specifications outlined in this company's request for bids. You believe this may offer opportunities for reaching a new market segment.

Preliminary investigations indicate that these types of contracts are issued to the lowest acceptable bidder unless there are unusual limiting circumstances. Several of your competitors are likely to bid on this contract. Your market information indicates that $365 per unit would be a competitive bid. One unknown factor of this opportunity is the effect it may have on your relationships with your current customers.

The advantages to you include increased volume, which might earn you better discounts from your manufacturer. In addition, success in this venture would make it easier to bid on other similar contracts. This strategy will result in extremely narrow profit margins and a change in your normal channels of distribution. In addition, you must order inventory before final acceptance of the bid in order to meet the delivery specifications of the contract.

What action should your division take?

1. Do not bid on this particular contract, but investigate other opportunities for the future.
2. Bid on the business. The cost of the proposal, $5,000, will be added to Other Expenses. (You must order 2,000 additional units now.)
3. Reject the idea of selling to this type of store at this time.

Enter your decision (1, 2, or 3) on the decision form.

Class discussion point: What are the tangible and intangible costs and benefits of entering this new market niche?

INCIDENT 6

A competitor has announced a new warranty policy: full warranty, no questions asked, for 180 days from the date of purchase. Your existing policy, modeled on the industry standard, is a limited 90-day warranty that can be enacted by drop-off service at any authorized dealer. Because warranties are an intangible benefit that enhance the features of a product package, consumers often make their purchasing decisions on the basis of a warranty. Focus group research indicates that your target market views the warranty policy as an important feature.

Your R & D department reports that the frequency of free repair is already at a high level and that it would be costly to extend the free-service component. A review of articles in trade magazines has cited your product for good quality control; however, market information indicates that some of your competitors will follow the lead of the major company that has implemented the extended warranty policy. How should your division respond?

1. Do some additional marketing research to see how important the feature really is.
2. Continue your present policy and begin an advertising campaign that highlights the quality of your product.
3. Do nothing at the present time until the market situation is clearer.
4. Increase the warranty to 180 days. Other Expenses charged: $100,000 for the first year of this new extended warranty as a reserve against additional future costs.
5. Maintain your 90-day policy but sell service contracts to provide insured maintenance when the warranty expires.

Enter your decision (1, 2, 3, 4, or 5) on the decision form.

Class discussion point: To what extent has the consumer movement affected warranty policies in the United States? Is it wise for a firm to go beyond the current industry warranty standard? What are the implications (especially for product quality) of doing so?

INCIDENT 7

The quarterly sales reports indicate an increase in requests from potential customers for a "store" or private-label audio system. This is a unique strategy for your industry and presents opportunities for volume sales in new outlets. Because of your manufacturing arrangements, you are limited to providing a sound system identical to your branded system, so the product would be clearly identifiable as yours to the sophisticated buyer.

Informal conversations with your distributors indicate that some retailers are unhappy with this and may look for another product if you offer a private-label product in addition to your own brand. Other retailers recognize that the look-alike feature will enable them to promote the benefit package offered by their outlet with some spin-off effect from the advertising of the private labeler.

It appears likely that your sales volume will increase if you pursue this route, but the resulting price structure would reduce your per unit profit for the unbranded system. The costs and benefits are difficult to calculate accurately. What decision should your team make?

1. Continue your present distribution. Encourage the outlets that want the private label to purchase in volume through their distributor cooperative.
2. Have your sales force survey actual and potential customers. Use this information to develop a cost-benefit analysis before making a final decision.
3. Pursue the private-label strategy as a complement to your existing distribution. The cost to initiate this new strategy is $50,000 (charged to Other Expenses).

Enter your decision (1, 2, or 3) on the decision form.

Class discussion point: If private labeling is a current industry practice, what factors must a firm consider in making this change in distribution/product strategy? Does a firm have a responsibility to protect the members of its distribution channels?

INCIDENT 8

"Our sales force is just a group of highly paid order takers," exploded your sales manager. "I just spent a week in each region, and all they do is take the orders from the distributors and purchasing agents. The consumers know more about our product than our salespeople do!"

"Do you think this is limiting the growth of sales?" a team member asked.

"It may be having some impact on obtaining sales in cases where the distributor has the option of several products. We have to be able to distinguish ours from others that appear to be similar," the sales manager responded.

"We may need to expand our training for the sales force and provide some training for the dealers as well, so that their salespeople can help a customer distinguish our outstanding features," another team member volunteered.

How should you respond to the above?

a. Hire an experienced salesperson trainer to ride with each salesperson for a two-week period to give him or her on-the-job training and store personnel on-site training. The cost is $50,000 per year.
b. Contract, as soon as possible, with a professional sales-training firm to conduct a week-long training workshop. If retailers want to send someone to the program, they could do so at their own expense. It will cost $25,000 to bring your sales force in for this training.
c. Plan to conduct two days of training in conjunction with the next annual sales meeting (scheduled to be held in six months). This will save the cost of bringing the sales force together twice this fiscal year. Cost: $10,000.
d. Have a marketing staff person assemble a training handbook for the sales force and dealers. Cost: $2,000.
e. Publish a monthly training newsletter for your sales force and dealers. This would require some consultation fees with outside sales-training experts and would cost $6,000 a year.
f. Let the sales force work this out itself. After all, its members are all relatively new and so is the company. They probably have their hands full just developing new business.

(over)

Record on your decision form the decision number below that corresponds to the item or items you want to implement. The cost shown is an annual cost that will be charged to Other Expenses in this quarter.

Decision Number to Record	Item(s) Above	Cost
1	a	$50,000
2	b	25,000
3	c	10,000
4	d	2,000
5	e	6,000
6	a, d	52,000
7	a, e	56,000
8	b, d	27,000
9	b, e	31,000
10	c, d	12,000
11	c, e	16,000
12	f	0

Enter your decision (1 through 12) on the decision form.

Class discussion point: To what extent does training pay off? Isn't on-the-job training the crux of training? Is training a nontangible employee benefit? Can you really teach someone how to sell?

INCIDENT 9

Your marketing manager attended a seminar on marketing information systems at a prestigious university. Since his return, he has been reviewing the division's information-collection, -processing, and -reporting system for accuracy, timeliness, and relevance. He feels the following offer some possibilities in this important area:

a. Warranty registration cards have been coming in from purchasers since the firm's start-up but have not been tabulated in any manner. These cards contain many bits of data that could give profiles of consumers and their buying behavior. It would cost $5,000 annually to process these cards so the information could be accessed easily via computer.

b. The division received a proposal from a software vendor to computerize all available market research information, including the data collected by your staff. This system, although costly, would integrate external market research with in-house data. Total one-time cost is $20,000.

c. There are several subscription electronic data bases that can be accessed through your in-house computer. These services provide environmental information as well as abstracts and articles from literally hundreds of business and marketing publications. The cost of this service annually, including equipment to interface with the host computer, is $5,000.

d. The sales force has the ability to collect useful information for a marketing information system but as yet there is no quick way to gather, analyze, and distribute this information. The first-year cost of placing these data into the division's computer for immediate access by all salespersons and managers is $10,000; updating in subsequent years would cost less.

e. Put this aspect of marketing on the back burner for now.

The development of a marketing information system is useful, but the method of implementation would have to be studied carefully for costs and benefits. Effective marketing information systems can have a direct effect on sales, especially if they are fully integrated with the company's entire information system. Which of the actions listed above should your firm take?

(over)

Record on your decision form the decision number below that corresponds to the item or items you want to implement. Costs will be charged to Other Expenses.

Decision Number to Record	Item(s) Above	Cost
1	a	$ 5,000
2	b	20,000
3	c	5,000
4	d	10,000
5	a, b	25,000
6	a, c	10,000
7	a, d	15,000
8	b, c	25,000
9	b, d	30,000
10	c, d	15,000
11	a, b, c	30,000
12	b, c, d	35,000
13	a, b, c, d	40,000
14	e	0

Enter your decision (1 through 14) on the decision form.

Class discussion point: When is the cost of information greater than the benefit? Is the need for more and better information increasing? Why or why not? What is the most important source of information for a marketing firm?

INCIDENT 10

The management team has just returned from a quarterly evaluation meeting at corporate headquarters. One of the items on the agenda was a proposal for you to contract for services from the Corporate Research Center. Pure research or "think tank" activities provide tangible and intangible benefits to a company. Most of the end products are marketing enhancements for product lines, provided to customers at no charge. Pure or developmental research may also extend the life cycle of a product. This is reflected in promotion strategies that advertise a "new improved Brand X."

Occasionally, a pure research facility develops a totally new product with substantial market potential. Although the chances of this happening are less than 1 in 10, the payoffs in new sales or licensing fees can be greater than 50 to 1. Your current R & D efforts are directed at technical service and quality control. However, your R & D manager believes that high-tech research would be of great value in the turbulent technological environment surrounding the home entertainment industry.

The corporate proposal will cost $100,000 annually. The return on investment cannot be estimated accurately. What response should you make?

1. Accept the corporate proposal. The cost, $100,000, will be allocated over the next four periods and charged to Other Expenses.
2. Ask your R & D manager to allocate 20 percent of her budget to this type of activity. Wait and see if it looks promising.
3. Use advertising and promotion to enhance and extend your product.
4. Continue with your present strategies.

Enter your decision (1, 2, 3, or 4) on the decision form.

Class discussion point: What are the costs and benefits of being a follower? A leader? Are think tank–type activities and pure research useless activities outside a university setting?

INCIDENT 11

The Association of Allied Consumer Electronics has sent a brochure to you outlining services to member organizations. The first service of interest is AACE-PAC, a separately funded political action organization that has a paid lobbyist to influence legislation affecting the electronics industry.

AACE-PAC has had two major successes: It promoted a section of the latest tax law, which allows audiovisual equipment to be deducted as an educational expense in certain situations; and it helped stop increased tariffs on value-added goods being shipped from Japan. Both of these pieces of legislation provided substantial intangible benefits to your firm and its customers. AACE-PAC is requesting $10,000 in support from member organizations to continue its activities effectively.

The second service provided by the association that is of interest to your firm is a research bureau. This office publishes bulletins and research studies concerning various aspects of your industry and its products. The bureau has just completed a comprehensive study of consumer buying behavior throughout the home electronics industry. You and most of your competitors have been unsuccessful in analyzing the buying behavior of stereo component owners, so this study may help you implement your marketing variables more efficiently. The cost of this report is $10,000, which includes an annual supplement.

Which services should your team purchase?

1. Subscribe to the Consumer Behavior Report of the research bureau. The cost, $10,000, will be charged to Other Expenses.
2. Join AACE-PAC. The cost, $10,000, will be charged to Other Expenses.
3. Take advantage of both services because the association has always provided a high level of member services. The cost, $20,000, will be charged to Other Expenses.
4. Do nothing at this time.

Enter your decision (1, 2, 3, or 4) on the decision form.

Class discussion point: Is there a payoff for industry activities? Does a firm have a responsibility to be involved in its industry association?

INCIDENT 12

A component of the annual review process for your organization is the development of new strategies for marketing operations. Your management team is having a brainstorming session, and, as the meeting unfolds, you hear many new ideas being generated. Any idea that is adopted will have to be turned into operative objectives. Few companies accomplish all of their objectives: The rule of thumb is that 80 percent of time and resources are spent on 20 percent of objectives.

This is a partial list of potential objectives generated by your team:

1. Open a company-owned store to test out the possibility of expanding vertically forward in the distribution chain.
2. Develop an all-new point-of-sale showroom display for your product with flashy electronic visuals.
3. Provide exclusive territories for dealers in order to develop brand loyalty.
4. Develop a network of sales through university outlets.
5. Co-sponsor concerts in key communities to raise awareness of your company in the audio entertainment market.
6. Contract with a hot-air balloon company to tour the country and compete in as many balloon races as possible with a balloon carrying your logo.

Create as many new alternatives as you can. Rank the entire list, keeping the 80-20 rule in mind and giving a rationalization for your ranking. This is not recorded on the decision form. Turn this in to your instructor.

Class discussion point: Is there any reason for planning beyond the very short term in a turbulent competitive environment? To what extent should a firm diversify into areas in which it has little expertise?

4

LOG OF QUARTERLY DECISIONS

As your firm makes decisions through the simulation, you may need to alter your strategy to meet competitive and/or economic changes. We recommend that you record your actions each quarter *and* the rationale for your decisions on these forms. You then will have a record to help you fine-tune your future decisions. Keep a copy of the actual numbers you input on Forms 2A, 2B, and 2C in Chapter 7.

LOG OF QUARTERLY DECISIONS

COMPANY NO. _____ PERIOD NO. _____

Decision: _____
_____
_____

Rationale: _____
_____
_____
_____

Decision: _____
_____
_____

Rationale: _____
_____
_____
_____

Decision: _____
_____
_____

Rationale: _____
_____
_____
_____

Decision: _____
_____
_____

Rationale: _____
_____
_____
_____

Decision: _____
_____
_____

Rationale: _____
_____
_____
_____

LOG OF QUARTERLY DECISIONS

COMPANY NO. _____ PERIOD NO. _____

Decision: _____
_____
_____

Rationale: _____
_____
_____
_____

Decision: _____
_____
_____

Rationale: _____
_____
_____
_____

Decision: _____
_____
_____

Rationale: _____
_____
_____
_____

Decision: _____
_____
_____

Rationale: _____
_____
_____
_____

Decision: _____
_____
_____

Rationale: _____
_____
_____
_____

LOG OF QUARTERLY DECISIONS

COMPANY NO. _____ PERIOD NO. _____

Decision: _____
_____
_____

Rationale: _____
_____
_____
_____

Decision: _____
_____
_____

Rationale: _____
_____
_____
_____

Decision: _____
_____
_____

Rationale: _____
_____
_____
_____

Decision: _____
_____
_____

Rationale: _____
_____
_____
_____

Decision: _____
_____
_____

Rationale: _____
_____
_____
_____

LOG OF QUARTERLY DECISIONS

COMPANY NO. _____ PERIOD NO. _____

Decision: _____
_____
_____

Rationale: _____
_____
_____
_____

Decision: _____
_____
_____

Rationale: _____
_____
_____
_____

Decision: _____
_____
_____

Rationale: _____
_____
_____
_____

Decision: _____
_____
_____

Rationale: _____
_____
_____
_____

Decision: _____
_____
_____

Rationale: _____
_____
_____
_____

LOG OF QUARTERLY DECISIONS

COMPANY NO. _____ PERIOD NO. _____

Decision: _____
_____
_____

Rationale: _____
_____
_____
_____

Decision: _____
_____
_____

Rationale: _____
_____
_____
_____

Decision: _____
_____
_____

Rationale: _____
_____
_____
_____

Decision: _____
_____
_____

Rationale: _____
_____
_____
_____

Decision: _____
_____
_____

Rationale: _____
_____
_____
_____

LOG OF QUARTERLY DECISIONS

COMPANY NO. _____ PERIOD NO. _____

Decision: _____
_____
_____

Rationale: _____
_____
_____
_____

Decision: _____
_____
_____

Rationale: _____
_____
_____
_____

Decision: _____
_____
_____

Rationale: _____
_____
_____
_____

Decision: _____
_____
_____

Rationale: _____
_____
_____

Decision: _____
_____
_____

Rationale: _____
_____
_____
_____

LOG OF QUARTERLY DECISIONS

COMPANY NO. _____ PERIOD NO. _____

Decision: _____
_____
_____

Rationale: _____
_____
_____
_____

Decision: _____
_____
_____

Rationale: _____
_____
_____
_____

Decision: _____
_____
_____

Rationale: _____
_____
_____
_____

Decision: _____
_____
_____

Rationale: _____
_____
_____
_____

Decision: _____
_____
_____

Rationale: _____
_____
_____
_____

LOG OF QUARTERLY DECISIONS

COMPANY NO. _____ PERIOD NO. _____

Decision: _____
_____
_____

Rationale: _____
_____
_____
_____

Decision: _____
_____
_____

Rationale: _____
_____
_____
_____

Decision: _____
_____
_____

Rationale: _____
_____
_____
_____

Decision: _____
_____
_____

Rationale: _____
_____
_____
_____

Decision: _____
_____
_____

Rationale: _____
_____
_____
_____

5

INTERNAL MARKETING
AUDIT AND PEER EVALUATION

The purpose of a marketing audit is to review your team's results at any given point during the simulation. This will help your team optimize future decisions. See Form A-1 on page 77. The peer evaluation is designed to give a performance evaluation to each team member. It is usually handed in to the instructor at mid-term and at the end of the term.

INTERNAL MARKETING AUDIT

A marketing audit is a comprehensive, systematic, periodic examination of a company's marketing environment, strategies, objectives, and activities with a view to determining opportunities and problem areas. The results should lead to recommendations for improving the company's marketing performance.

Your instructor may want this audit made sometime during the halfway point of play or after the simulation ends. Even if it is not a required activity, your team should evaluate its actions at least once during the simulation in order to ascertain if you have been choosing the most appropriate actions. This is a good example of the control function of marketing management. You have planned your objectives for the simulation, organized the resources of your management team and of the simulation division, made decisions in directing the activities, and to some extent controlled the firm through financial analysis. At this point, it would be wise to make a thorough quantitative and qualitative evaluation of (1) your management team (even though it may only be yourself!) and (2) your simulation division.

To emphasize the point: The purpose of the audit is to have you review your results through a particular quarter of play, compare them with your thinking when the simulation started, and make any changes you feel are necessary to improve your team's performance and your own learning. If the audit comes during the midpoint of the simulation, you still have time to take corrective action. If the audit is done at the simulation's end, your conclusions will be more in the form of a report card as to your success. A key point in the latter case is the response to the question "If you had the opportunity to start all over again, what would you do differently?" The audit guide included in this section is just that—a guide. There are other questions and approaches to this activity. Just remember that the audit is not a typical accounting audit but rather a management audit and should be approached as such.

Some other approaches and topics that could be involved in looking at your team and company operations include the following:

1. Select one area that you feel presents a major problem for your team. It may be a lack of sales or, conversely, frequent stock-outs of the product. It could be a matter of not understanding the interrelationships among prices, marketing activities, and sales. These are just a few examples; there are certainly others. Analyze the problem, present alternative

solutions, and select the solution that you will (or would) implement in order to improve your company's performance from this point forward.

2. If your team has more than one person, you could select a major area in which your team is having a problem and work out a strategy for solving that problem. One example may be the need to communicate effectively with one another to maximize your understanding of one another's views. Another team issue may be how to make group decisions better (with fewer disagreements). Still another may be to admit that one or more of the group members need to develop a better understanding of the components of income and expense on your printout.

3. Review the log of quarterly decisions for all quarters up to the present. Do these records clearly indicate the rationale for the decisions you have made in past quarters? Have you made assumptions that are no longer valid? Do your records support your actions?

4. Review your initial mission statement, objectives, and policies. Ask yourself these questions:

   a. What was our original strategy? Are we still on course?
   b. Are we achieving our objectives? If not, why not? What changes can we make to improve the possibilities of achieving our goals?
   c. Can we measure the progress we are making (or have made) toward achieving our objectives? If not, can we restate our objectives in more specific terms so that we can determine whether we have achieved our objectives at some future measuring point?
   d. Are our policies helping us to achieve our objectives? Are we following policies even though they are not formally stated? Should we clarify what we are doing by thinking through these unwritten policies and formally writing them out? Are we utilizing all of our original policies? Should some be updated? Changed?
   e. Are we following the strategies we initially established? Do we need new strategies?

5. If you are doing this audit during simulation play, you may want to consider the following idea. Revise the interpersonal roles you each play within your team. For example, if one person is the low-keyed nonverbal type, he or she may be encouraged to play a more active role. Of course, the talkers of the team will need to take a more passive role and listen more attentively. The object is to try to participate in a manner that is not your normal pattern and to experience your feelings about being in this different role.

The key element of the audit is to learn something about yourself, your company, the marketplace, or the environment that will help you understand the real world in a more effective manner. The audit will cover six areas of the marketing situation: the environment; the marketing mission, strategies, and objectives; the organizational structure; marketing information systems; marketing profitability; and the marketing mix. It should produce some short- and long-run recommendations that lead to improved performance.

FORM A-1: MARKETING AUDIT

COMPANY NO. _____ PERIOD NO._____

PREPARED BY _____

1. Is the mission of the division stated in market-oriented terms?

2. Are the objectives stated in the form of clear goals to guide marketing planning and subsequent performance measurement?

3. What is the core marketing strategy for achieving the objectives? Is it a sound marketing strategy?

4. What major environmental forces pose opportunities and threats for the division?

5. Has the division taken any action in response to these developments and trends?

6. Who are our major competitors? What are their strengths and weaknesses?

7. What is happening to the market size, growth trends, and profits? How does this position the product in terms of life cycle analysis?

8. Are marketing responsibilities structured well? Are we employing the optimal organizational structure for marketing this product?

9. Are there any groups within our organization or in the channels that need training or motivation? What level of resources should we allocate for this purpose?

10. Is the marketing intelligence system, including market research efforts, producing accurate, timely, and sufficient information about developments in the marketplace?

11. Is there a mechanism for examining and validating the level of marketing expenses? Do any of the activities seem to have excessive costs?

12. Are the objectives for each of the marketing variables (advertising, sales promotion, distribution, product improvement, price, and sales force) justifiable and sound?

13. Are the control procedures on a quarterly basis adequate to ensure that marketing plan objectives are being achieved?

14. Are ordering policies effective (is an optimal level of inventory on hand each quarter)?

15. Are our objectives, strategies, and policies positioning us for the intermediate and/or long run, or only for the short run?

Other Notes Concerning the Marketing Audit:

FORM B-1: EXECUTIVE BONUS RECOMMENDATION

COMPANY NO. _____

QUARTER NO. _____   PREPARED BY _____

As a member of your company's Executive Compensation Committee, you have been assigned the task of allocating $50,000 among the managers.

Note: A fair, firm, and objective performance evaluation is a crucial managerial function. Although peer evaluation is not easy, your instructor expects you to complete this task honestly.

Fill in the names of the executives   Fill in the amount of
in your firm, including your own: the executive bonus:

_____ $ _____

_____ $ _____

_____ $ _____

_____ $ _____

_____ $ _____

                              TOTAL $ 50,000

FORM B-2: MARKETING SIMULATION PEER EVALUATION

QUARTER NO. _____   COMPANY NO. _____

The purpose of this analysis is to give credit to those students who went the "extra mile" or who did their fair share of the simulation work. Conversely, if any team member did not do his or her fair share (for whatever reason), that student should not get full credit for the simulation work. Be assured that all data on this form will be held in confidence.

PERFORMANCE EVALUATION IS AN IMPORTANT PART OF EVERY MANAGER'S JOB; YOUR INSTRUCTOR EXPECTS YOU TO MAKE A FAIR AND ACCURATE EVALUATION.

Your name on the first line:	Attendance & Cooperation (5, 4, 3, 2, 1)	Academic Contribution (5, 4, 3, 2, 1)	Overall Comparative Ranking (5, 4, 3, 2, 1)	Total Points
	(Do not grade yourself, but do rank yourself.)		_____	
_____	_____	_____	_____	_____
_____	_____	_____	_____	_____
_____	_____	_____	_____	_____
_____	_____	_____	_____	_____

Add the points from the three columns and place in the total points column.

Key to Numerical Ranking

Attendance & Cooperation

5 = Was a team leader both in and out of class; cooperation superior.
4 = Attended meetings regularly; good cooperation; a team player.
3 = Attended meetings fairly regularly; did what was asked but no more.
2 = Missed some meetings and did the minimum amount of work.
1 = Poor attendance at meetings and/or poor cooperation and work share.

(over)

Academic Contribution

5 = A team leader in ideas; enthusiastic; a lot of good ideas.
4 = Contributed greatly to the team; did more than his or her fair share.
3 = Had good ideas from time to time; an average performance.
2 = Probably was either too quiet or not interested enough to be an effective academic contributor to the team.
1 = Contributed little to the team.

Overall Comparative Ranking

5 = The team leader (or *a* team leader, if more than one).
4 = A team player, second to the leader(s), but only slightly; excellent work.
3 = An average member of the team.
2 = Slightly below average member of the team.
1 = Contributed least to the team.

6

BREAKEVEN ANALYSIS

Breakeven analysis is a method of determining the minimum sales volume required to cover all costs at a given price level. A more detailed explanation and worksheets are included in this chapter.

In order to help establish prices, a company must analyze demand, cost, and profit relationships. One method of doing this is breakeven volume analysis. The point at which the cost of producing and marketing a product equals the revenues from selling it is called the *breakeven point*. In order to determine the breakeven point, it is necessary to separate the fixed costs of operations from the variable costs associated with each unit of product. The result of these calculations answers two questions: What is the lowest level of production and sales that the division can make and not lose money? And what are the various profits that can be assumed for various levels of sales? To use this analysis effectively, breakeven volume should be calculated for several levels of prices.

There are two methods for approaching the breakeven problem. One is the algebraic method and the other is the graphic method. Both are described in detail to allow your division to use the tool effectively in making quality decisions. For the purposes of the simulation, fixed costs include all marketing expenses and overhead expenses. Variable costs are the unit cost of goods sold.

ALGEBRAIC BREAKEVEN

The algebraic breakeven formula is as follows:

$$\frac{\text{Total fixed costs}}{\text{Current unit price} - \text{cost of each unit sold}}$$

It is often difficult to determine which costs are fixed and which costs are variable. A rule of thumb is to plot each component to see if the cost has an increment for each unit of product or service. The customary variable costs are raw materials, direct labor, freight, and variable overhead expenses (for example, electricity for production machinery). All other costs would be considered fixed for the breakeven analysis.

Using the data from the Quarter 0 printout (page 25), the following would be obtained:

$$\frac{\text{Total fixed costs}}{\text{Contribution margin per unit}} = \frac{\text{All expenses except cost of goods sold}}{\text{Unit price} - \text{unit cost of goods sold}}$$

$$\frac{\$368,300}{\$500 - \$350} = 2,455 \text{ units}$$

The breakeven point is 2,455 units at this price and cost level. This can be interpreted to mean that if prices and expenses remain constant, your division must sell 2,455 units before it will begin making a profit. Marketing strategies should be aimed at penetrating the market so that demand exceeds this level.

GRAPHIC BREAKEVEN

Graphic breakeven analysis gives a pictorial representation of the relationships between costs and profits. Potential profits and losses can be determined quickly for each level of sales at a given price and cost level. Marketers are concerned with relevant ranges of operations, and the graphic representation of breakeven provides a tool for mapping this concept. The graph in Figure 6.1 shows the breakeven chart for Period 0. There are additional forms provided so that you can chart this information for each decision made by your team.

FIGURE 6.1 GRAPHIC BREAKEVEN ANALYSIS

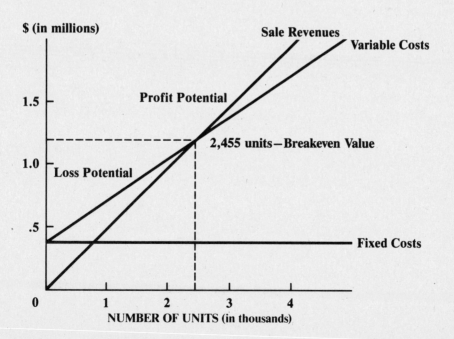

FORM BE-1: BREAKEVEN ANALYSIS

COMPANY NO. _____ PERIOD NO. _____

PREPARED BY _____

REVENUES & COSTS
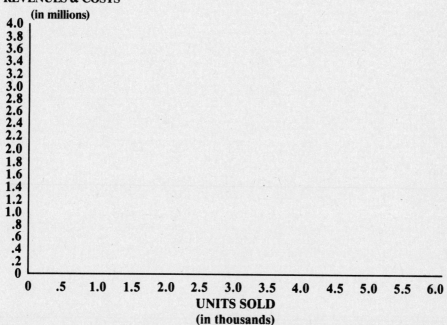
(in millions)

Y-axis: 4.0, 3.8, 3.6, 3.4, 3.2, 3.0, 2.8, 2.6, 2.4, 2.2, 2.0, 1.8, 1.6, 1.4, 1.2, 1.0, .8, .6, .4, .2, 0

X-axis: 0 .5 1.0 1.5 2.0 2.5 3.0 3.5 4.0 4.5 5.0 5.5 6.0

UNITS SOLD
(in thousands)

Breakeven Formula:

$$\frac{\text{Total fixed costs}^*}{\text{Current price} - \text{variable cost}^\dagger} = \underline{\qquad\qquad} = \underline{\qquad\qquad} \text{ units}$$

*In this simulation, *fixed costs* are defined as selling expenses plus overhead expenses.
†Same as unit cost of goods sold.

FORM BE-1: BREAKEVEN ANALYSIS

COMPANY NO. _____ PERIOD NO. _____

PREPARED BY _____

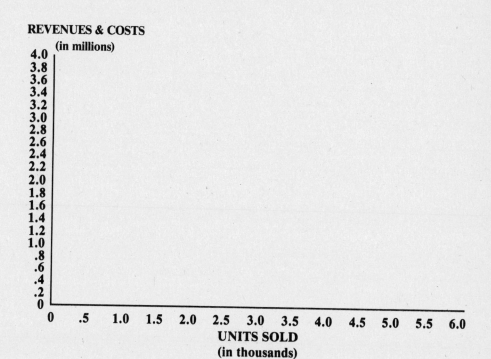

REVENUES & COSTS
(in millions)

UNITS SOLD
(in thousands)

Breakeven Formula:

$$\frac{\text{Total fixed costs}^*}{\text{Current price} - \text{variable cost}^\dagger} = \underline{\hspace{2cm}} = \underline{\hspace{2cm}} \text{ units}$$

*In this simulation, *fixed costs* are defined as selling expenses plus overhead expenses.
†Same as unit cost of goods sold.

FORM BE-1: BREAKEVEN ANALYSIS

COMPANY NO. _____ PERIOD NO. _____

PREPARED BY _____

REVENUES & COSTS

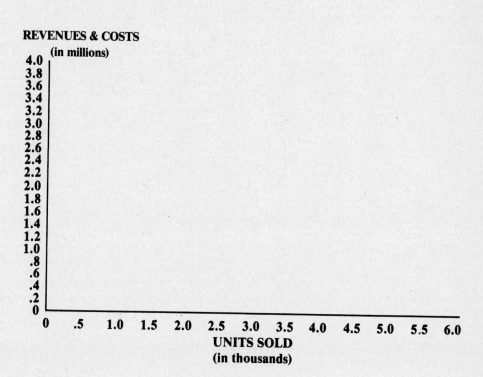

Breakeven Formula:

$$\frac{\text{Total fixed costs}^{*}}{\text{Current price} - \text{variable cost}^{\dagger}} = \underline{\hspace{2cm}} = \underline{\hspace{2cm}} \text{ units}$$

*In this simulation, *fixed costs* are defined as selling expenses plus overhead expenses.
†Same as unit cost of goods sold.

FORM BE-1: BREAKEVEN ANALYSIS

COMPANY NO. ＿＿＿＿ PERIOD NO. ＿＿＿

PREPARED BY ＿＿＿＿＿＿＿＿＿＿＿

REVENUES & COSTS

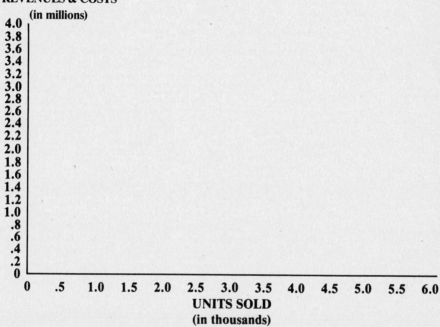

UNITS SOLD
(in thousands)

Breakeven Formula:

$$\frac{\text{Total fixed costs}^*}{\text{Current price} - \text{variable cost}^\dagger} = \underline{\hspace{3cm}} = \underline{\hspace{3cm}} \text{ units}$$

---

*In this simulation, *fixed costs* are defined as selling expenses plus overhead expenses.
†Same as unit cost of goods sold.

7

MANAGEMENT
INFORMATION

This chapter contains several different types of forms and charts to help your team organize and maintain the management information it needs to make better-informed decisions.

FORM OB-1: CORPORATE MISSION, OBJECTIVES, AND STRATEGY

Corporate Mission (or purpose): _____

_____

Objective #1: _____

    Strategy (or Action Plan) to accomplish this objective: _____

    _____

    _____

    Policy (or policies) to aid in implementing this objective: _____

    _____

    _____

Objective #2: _____

    Strategy (or Action Plan) to accomplish this objective: _____

    _____

    _____

    Policy (or policies) to aid in implementing this objective: _____

    _____

    _____

Objective #3: _____

    Strategy (or Action Plan) to accomplish this objective: _____

    _____

    _____

Note: This form is illustrative of the hierarchy of corporate planning. It should be amended as necessary for planning within your own firm.

Policy (or policies) to aid in implementing this objective: _____

_____

_____

Objective #4: _____

    Strategy (or Action Plan) to accomplish this objective: _____

    _____

    _____

    Policy (or policies) to aid in implementing this objective: _____

    _____

    _____

Objective #5: _____

    Strategy (or Action Plan) to accomplish this objective: _____

    _____

    _____

    Policy (or policies) to aid in implementing this objective: _____

    _____

    _____

Objective #6: _____

    Strategy (or Action Plan) to accomplish this objective: _____

    _____

    _____

    Policy (or policies) to aid in implementing this objective: _____

    _____

    _____

FORM P-1: DIVISION POLICIES

INDUSTRY _____ COMPANY NO. _____

A selected group of policy areas are listed below for your team's considera-
tion. Try to write one or two for each area.

1. Advertising

2. Advertising Budget

3. Sales Promotion

4. Sales Promotion Budget

5. Pricing

6. Inventory Level/Ordering

7. Market/Customer Development

8. Customer Service/Warranty

9. Product Development/Research/Innovation

10. Sales Force (levels, training, compensation, duties)

11. Social Responsibility/Public Image/Environment

FORM 2A: RECORD OF QUARTERLY DECISIONS AND MARKETING DATA ANALYSIS

PRODUCT 1

Period Number	Price	Advertising Budget	Promotion Budget	Dist. Budget	Bonus Paid	R & D Budget	# Sales-persons	Sales (units)
-2	530	70,000	30,000	10,000	0	20,000	4	3,659
-1	520	50,000	50,000	10,000	0	20,000	5	3,703
0	500	50,000	30,000	10,000	0	20,000	5	4,077
1								
2								
3								
4								
5								
6								
7								
8								
9								
10								
11								
12								

FORM 2B: RECORD OF QUARTERLY DECISIONS AND MARKETING DATA ANALYSIS

PRODUCT 2

Period Number	Price	Advertising Budget	Promotion Budget	Dist. Budget	Bonus Paid	R & D Budget	# Sales-persons	Sales (units)
0	This product was not sold in Period 0							
1								
2								
3								
4								
5								
6								
7								
8								
9								
10								
11								
12								

FORM 2C: RECORD OF QUARTERLY DECISIONS AND MARKETING DATA ANALYSIS

OTHER DECISIONS

Period Number	Salespersons Hired	Marketing Research Studies Ordered (Place Study #s)	Products Ordered (units)	Administrative Costs	Incident Response #
0	0	1	4,500	200,000	n/a
1					
2					
3					
4					
5					
6					
7					
8					
9					
10					
11					
12					

FORM 3: INVENTORY MANAGEMENT WORKSHEET

Period Number	Goods Ordered (col. 1)	Goods Rec'd. & Accepted (col. 2)	% Shrinkage (col. 1 - col. 2 ÷ col. 2)	Beg. Inv. (col. 4)	Units Sold (col. 5)	Ending Inv. (col. 2 + col. 4 - col. 5)	Per Unit Cost*
-2	4,211	4,047		0	3,659	388	
-1	3,600	3,500		388	3,703	185	
0	4,500	4,254		189	4,077	365	
1							
2							
3							
4							
5							
6							
7							
8							
9							
10							
11							
12							

*Per unit cost = (units in beg. inv. × unit price) + (units rec'd. and accepted × unit price) ÷ total units.

FORM 4: DEMAND ELASTICITY ANALYSIS

Demand elasticity is a determination of the sensitivity of quantity with respect to price. It is determined by plotting the quantity of the product on the x axis, the price of the product sold on the y axis, then calculating the percentage change in the slope (the change in the rise divided by the change in the run). The formula:

$$\frac{\dfrac{P_n - P_{n-1}}{P_n}}{\dfrac{Q_n - Q_{n-1}}{Q_n}}$$

P_n and P_{n-1} are the prices for this quarter and the previous quarter; Q_n and Q_{n-1} are the demand for this quarter and the previous quarter. Relatively elastic demand is characterized by higher responsiveness to a change in price. Relatively inelastic demand is characterized by a lack of responsiveness to a change in price. Use the table below to chart unit prices, sales, and an estimate of the demand elasticity for your industry or firm.

Period	Unit Price	Volume Sold	Elasticity
n – 1	$520	3,703	
0	500	4,077	–2.6
1			
2			
3			
4			
5			
6			
7			
8			
9			

Period	Unit Price	Volume Sold	Elasticity
10			
11			
12			

8

WORKSHEETS AND
DECISION FORMS

This chapter contains multiple copies of five different worksheets as well as the quarterly decision forms.

FORM 5: SELECTED FINANCIAL RATIOS

COMPANY NO. ____ PERIOD NO. ____

PREPARED BY _____

1. Inventory Turnover

$$\frac{\text{Cost of goods sold}}{\text{Ending inventory \$}} = \text{_____} = \text{_____}$$

2. Gross Profit Margin

$$\frac{\text{Sales (Prod. 1) - cost of goods sold}}{\text{Sales (Prod. 1)}} = \text{_____} = \text{_____}$$

$$\frac{\text{Sales (Prod. 2) - cost of goods sold}}{\text{Sales (Prod. 2)}} = \text{_____} = \text{_____}$$

3. Return on Sales

$$\frac{\text{Net contribution (Product 1)}}{\text{Sales (Product 1)}} = \text{_____} = \text{_____}$$

$$\frac{\text{Net contribution (Product 2)}}{\text{Sales (Product 2)}} = \text{_____} = \text{_____}$$

4. Return on Assets

$$\frac{\text{Contribution to corp. overhead*}}{\text{Assets in this division}} = \text{_____} = \text{_____}$$

*This figure does not have any tax liability in it. In order to make the ratio more meaningful, this figure should be reduced by 50% for various income and other tax expenses.

FORM 5: SELECTED FINANCIAL RATIOS

COMPANY NO. _____ PERIOD NO. _____

PREPARED BY _____

1. Inventory Turnover

$$\frac{\text{Cost of goods sold}}{\text{Ending inventory \$}} = \text{_____} = \text{_____}$$

2. Gross Profit Margin

$$\frac{\text{Sales (Prod. 1)} - \text{cost of goods sold}}{\text{Sales (Prod. 1)}} = \text{_____} = \text{_____}$$

$$\frac{\text{Sales (Prod. 2)} - \text{cost of goods sold}}{\text{Sales (Prod. 2)}} = \text{_____} = \text{_____}$$

3. Return on Sales

$$\frac{\text{Net contribution (Product 1)}}{\text{Sales (Product 1)}} = \text{_____} = \text{_____}$$

$$\frac{\text{Net contribution (Product 2)}}{\text{Sales (Product 2)}} = \text{_____} = \text{_____}$$

4. Return on Assets

$$\frac{\text{Contribution to corp. overhead*}}{\text{Assets in this division}} = \text{_____} = \text{_____}$$

*This figure does not have any tax liability in it. In order to make the ratio more meaningful, this figure should be reduced by 50% for various income and other tax expenses.

FORM 5: SELECTED FINANCIAL RATIOS

COMPANY NO. ____ PERIOD NO. ____

PREPARED BY _____

1. Inventory Turnover

$$\frac{\text{Cost of goods sold}}{\text{Ending inventory \$}} = \underline{\hspace{2cm}} = \underline{\hspace{2cm}}$$

2. Gross Profit Margin

$$\frac{\text{Sales (Prod. 1)} - \text{cost of goods sold}}{\text{Sales (Prod. 1)}} = \underline{\hspace{2cm}} = \underline{\hspace{2cm}}$$

$$\frac{\text{Sales (Prod. 2)} - \text{cost of goods sold}}{\text{Sales (Prod. 2)}} = \underline{\hspace{2cm}} = \underline{\hspace{2cm}}$$

3. Return on Sales

$$\frac{\text{Net contribution (Product 1)}}{\text{Sales (Product 1)}} = \underline{\hspace{2cm}} = \underline{\hspace{2cm}}$$

$$\frac{\text{Net contribution (Product 2)}}{\text{Sales (Product 2)}} = \underline{\hspace{2cm}} = \underline{\hspace{2cm}}$$

4. Return on Assets

$$\frac{\text{Contribution to corp. overhead*}}{\text{Assets in this division}} = \underline{\hspace{2cm}} = \underline{\hspace{2cm}}$$

*This figure does not have any tax liability in it. In order to make the ratio more meaningful, this figure should be reduced by 50% for various income and other tax expenses.

FORM 5: SELECTED FINANCIAL RATIOS

COMPANY NO. _____ PERIOD NO. _____

PREPARED BY _____

1. Inventory Turnover

$$\frac{\text{Cost of goods sold}}{\text{Ending inventory \$}} = \underline{\hspace{3cm}} = \underline{\hspace{2.5cm}}$$

2. Gross Profit Margin

$$\frac{\text{Sales (Prod. 1)} - \text{cost of goods sold}}{\text{Sales (Prod. 1)}} = \underline{\hspace{3cm}} = \underline{\hspace{2.5cm}}$$

$$\frac{\text{Sales (Prod. 2)} - \text{cost of goods sold}}{\text{Sales (Prod. 2)}} = \underline{\hspace{3cm}} = \underline{\hspace{2.5cm}}$$

3. Return on Sales

$$\frac{\text{Net contribution (Product 1)}}{\text{Sales (Product 1)}} = \underline{\hspace{3cm}} = \underline{\hspace{2.5cm}}$$

$$\frac{\text{Net contribution (Product 2)}}{\text{Sales (Product 2)}} = \underline{\hspace{3cm}} = \underline{\hspace{2.5cm}}$$

4. Return on Assets

$$\frac{\text{Contribution to corp. overhead*}}{\text{Assets in this division}} = \underline{\hspace{3cm}} = \underline{\hspace{2.5cm}}$$

*This figure does not have any tax liability in it. In order to make the ratio more meaningful, this figure should be reduced by 50% for various income and other tax expenses.

FORM 6: UNIT PROFIT AND COST ANALYSIS

COMPANY NO. _____ PERIOD NO. _____

PREPARED BY _____

	PRODUCT 1	PRODUCT 2
1. Current Selling Price	_____	_____
2. Unit Cost (from printout)	(−) _____	(−) _____
3. Contribution Margin	_____	_____

Marketing Variable Expenses

4. Advertising ÷ units sold	_____	_____
5. Sales Prom. ÷ units sold	_____	_____
6. Dist. Imprv. ÷ units sold	_____	_____
7. Bonus Paid ÷ units sold	_____	_____
8. R & D ÷ units sold	_____	_____
9. Total Marketing Expense	(−) _____	(−) _____
10. Contribution Margin	_____	_____

Overhead and Administrative Expense*

11. Sales Force ÷ units sold	_____	_____
12. Inv. Exp. ÷ units sold	_____	_____
13. Mkt. Res. ÷ units sold	_____	_____
14. Adm. Exp. ÷ units sold	_____	_____
15. Other Exp. ÷ units sold	_____	_____
16. Total O & A Expense	(−) _____	(−) _____
17. Unit Profit or Loss	_____	_____

*If you have two products, allocate the selling and administrative expenses by the percentage of total sales for each product. For example:

$$\frac{\text{Sales of product 1}}{\text{Total sales}} = \underline{\hspace{1cm}} \% \text{ for Product 1}$$

FORM 6: UNIT PROFIT AND COST ANALYSIS

COMPANY NO. _____ PERIOD NO. _____

PREPARED BY _____

	PRODUCT 1	PRODUCT 2
1. Current Selling Price	_____	_____
2. Unit Cost (from printout)	(−) _____	(−) _____
3. Contribution Margin	_____	_____

Marketing Variable Expenses

4. Advertising ÷ units sold	_____	_____
5. Sales Prom. ÷ units sold	_____	_____
6. Dist. Imprv. ÷ units sold	_____	_____
7. Bonus Paid ÷ units sold	_____	_____
8. R & D ÷ units sold	_____	_____
9. Total Marketing Expense	(−) _____	(−) _____
10. Contribution Margin	_____	_____

Overhead and Administrative Expense*

11. Sales Force ÷ units sold	_____	_____
12. Inv. Exp. ÷ units sold	_____	_____
13. Mkt. Res. ÷ units sold	_____	_____
14. Adm. Exp. ÷ units sold	_____	_____
15. Other Exp. ÷ units sold	_____	_____
16. Total O & A Expense	(−) _____	(−) _____
17. Unit Profit or Loss	_____	_____

*If you have two products, allocate the selling and administrative expenses by the percentage of total sales for each product. For example:

$$\frac{\text{Sales of product 1}}{\text{Total sales}} = \underline{\hspace{1cm}} \% \text{ for Product 1}$$

FORM 6: UNIT PROFIT AND COST ANALYSIS

COMPANY NO. _____ PERIOD NO. _____

PREPARED BY _____

	PRODUCT 1	**PRODUCT 2**
1. Current Selling Price	_____	_____
2. Unit Cost (from printout)	(−) _____	(−) _____
3. Contribution Margin	_____	_____

Marketing Variable Expenses

	PRODUCT 1	PRODUCT 2
4. Advertising ÷ units sold	_____	_____
5. Sales Prom. ÷ units sold	_____	_____
6. Dist. Imprv. ÷ units sold	_____	_____
7. Bonus Paid ÷ units sold	_____	_____
8. R & D ÷ units sold	_____	_____
9. Total Marketing Expense	(−) _____	(−) _____
10. Contribution Margin	_____	_____

*Overhead and Administrative Expense**

	PRODUCT 1	PRODUCT 2
11. Sales Force ÷ units sold	_____	_____
12. Inv. Exp. ÷ units sold	_____	_____
13. Mkt. Res. ÷ units sold	_____	_____
14. Adm. Exp. ÷ units sold	_____	_____
15. Other Exp. ÷ units sold	_____	_____
16. Total O & A Expense	(−) _____	(−) _____
17. Unit Profit or Loss	_____	_____

*If you have two products, allocate the selling and administrative expenses by the percentage of total sales for each product. For example:

$$\frac{\text{Sales of product 1}}{\text{Total sales}} = \underline{\hspace{1cm}}\% \text{ for Product 1}$$

FORM 6: UNIT PROFIT AND COST ANALYSIS

COMPANY NO. _____ PERIOD NO. _____

PREPARED BY _____

	PRODUCT 1	PRODUCT 2
1. Current Selling Price	_____	_____
2. Unit Cost (from printout)	(−) _____	(−) _____
3. Contribution Margin	_____	_____

Marketing Variable Expenses

	PRODUCT 1	PRODUCT 2
4. Advertising ÷ units sold	_____	_____
5. Sales Prom. ÷ units sold	_____	_____
6. Dist. Imprv. ÷ units sold	_____	_____
7. Bonus Paid ÷ units sold	_____	_____
8. R & D ÷ units sold	_____	_____
9. Total Marketing Expense	(−) _____	(−) _____
10. Contribution Margin	_____	_____

Overhead and Administrative Expense*

	PRODUCT 1	PRODUCT 2
11. Sales Force ÷ units sold	_____	_____
12. Inv. Exp. ÷ units sold	_____	_____
13. Mkt. Res. ÷ units sold	_____	_____
14. Adm. Exp. ÷ units sold	_____	_____
15. Other Exp. ÷ units sold	_____	_____
16. Total O & A Expense	(−) _____	(−) _____
17. Unit Profit or Loss	_____	_____

*If you have two products, allocate the selling and administrative expenses by the percentage of total sales for each product. For example:

$$\frac{\text{Sales of product 1}}{\text{Total sales}} = \underline{\hspace{1cm}} \% \text{ for Product 1}$$

FORM 7: PRO FORMA INCOME STATEMENT

COMPANY NO. ____ PERIOD NO. ____

PREPARED BY _____

	PROJECTION I	**PROJECTION II**
PRODUCT 1		
1. Projected Sales _____ units	_____	_____
2. Cost of Goods Sold (−)	_____	_____
3. Gross Profit Margin	_____	_____
PRODUCT 2		
4. Projected Sales _____ units	_____	_____
5. Cost of Goods Sold (−)	_____	_____
6. Gross Profit Margin	_____	_____
7. Gross Margin/both products	_____	_____
EXPENSES − Product 1		
8. Advertising	_____	_____
9. Sales Promotion	_____	_____
10. Dist. Imprv.	_____	_____
11. Bonus Cost	_____	_____
12. R & D	_____	_____
13. Total Exp. Product 1	_____	_____
14. Project Contribution of Prod. 1 (Line 3 − Line 13)	_____	_____
EXPENSES − Product 2		
15. Advertising	_____	_____
16. Sales Promotion	_____	_____
17. Dist. Imprv.	_____	_____
18. Bonus Cost	_____	_____
19. R & D	_____	_____
20. Total Exp. Product 2	_____	_____
21. Project Contribution of Prod. 2 (Line 6 − Line 20)	_____	_____
22. Gross Contrib./both prod. (Line 14 + Line 21)	_____	_____
OVERHEAD		
23. Sales Force Expenses	_____	_____
24. Sales Force Bonus	_____	_____
25. Inventory Expense	_____	_____
26. Marketing Research	_____	_____
27. Administrative Expense	_____	_____
28. Other Expenses	_____	_____
29. Total Overhead Expenses	_____	_____
30. Net Contribution (Line 22 − Line 29)	_____	_____

FORM 7: PRO FORMA INCOME STATEMENT

COMPANY NO. _____ PERIOD NO. _____

PREPARED BY _____

	PROJECTION I	PROJECTION II
PRODUCT 1		
1. Projected Sales _____ units	_____	_____
2. Cost of Goods Sold (−)	_____	_____
3. Gross Profit Margin	_____	_____
PRODUCT 2		
4. Projected Sales _____ units	_____	_____
5. Cost of Goods Sold (−)	_____	_____
6. Gross Profit Margin	_____	_____
7. Gross Margin/both products	_____	_____
EXPENSES − Product 1		
8. Advertising	_____	_____
9. Sales Promotion	_____	_____
10. Dist. Imprv.	_____	_____
11. Bonus Cost	_____	_____
12. R & D	_____	_____
13. Total Exp. Product 1	_____	_____
14. Project Contribution of Prod. 1 (Line 3 − Line 13)	_____	_____
EXPENSES − Product 2		
15. Advertising	_____	_____
16. Sales Promotion	_____	_____
17. Dist. Imprv.	_____	_____
18. Bonus Cost	_____	_____
19. R & D	_____	_____
20. Total Exp. Product 2	_____	_____
21. Project Contribution of Prod. 2 (Line 6 − Line 20)	_____	_____
22. Gross Contrib./both prod. (Line 14 + Line 21)	_____	_____
OVERHEAD		
23. Sales Force Expenses	_____	_____
24. Sales Force Bonus	_____	_____
25. Inventory Expense	_____	_____
26. Marketing Research	_____	_____
27. Administrative Expense	_____	_____
28. Other Expenses	_____	_____
29. Total Overhead Expenses	_____	_____
30. Net Contribution (Line 22 − Line 29)	_____	_____

FORM 7: PRO FORMA INCOME STATEMENT

COMPANY NO. _____ PERIOD NO. _____

PREPARED BY _____

	PROJECTION I	PROJECTION II
PRODUCT 1		
1. Projected Sales _____ units	_____	_____
2. Cost of Goods Sold (−)	_____	_____
3. Gross Profit Margin	_____	_____
PRODUCT 2		
4. Projected Sales _____ units	_____	_____
5. Cost of Goods Sold (−)	_____	_____
6. Gross Profit Margin	_____	_____
7. Gross Margin/both products	_____	_____
EXPENSES – Product 1		
8. Advertising	_____	_____
9. Sales Promotion	_____	_____
10. Dist. Imprv.	_____	_____
11. Bonus Cost	_____	_____
12. R & D	_____	_____
13. Total Exp. Product 1	_____	_____
14. Project Contribution of Prod. 1 (Line 3 − Line 13)	_____	_____
EXPENSES – Product 2		
15. Advertising	_____	_____
16. Sales Promotion	_____	_____
17. Dist. Imprv.	_____	_____
18. Bonus Cost	_____	_____
19. R & D	_____	_____
20. Total Exp. Product 2	_____	_____
21. Project Contribution of Prod. 2 (Line 6 − Line 20)	_____	_____
22. Gross Contrib./both prod. (Line 14 + Line 21)	_____	_____
OVERHEAD		
23. Sales Force Expenses	_____	_____
24. Sales Force Bonus	_____	_____
25. Inventory Expense	_____	_____
26. Marketing Research	_____	_____
27. Administrative Expense	_____	_____
28. Other Expenses	_____	_____
29. Total Overhead Expenses	_____	_____
30. Net Contribution (Line 22 − Line 29)	_____	_____

FORM 7: PRO FORMA INCOME STATEMENT

COMPANY NO. _____ PERIOD NO. _____

PREPARED BY _____

	PROJECTION I	PROJECTION II
PRODUCT 1		
1. Projected Sales _____ units	_____	_____
2. Cost of Goods Sold (−)	_____	_____
3. Gross Profit Margin	_____	_____
PRODUCT 2		
4. Projected Sales _____ units	_____	_____
5. Cost of Goods Sold (−)	_____	_____
6. Gross Profit Margin	_____	_____
7. Gross Margin/both products	_____	_____
EXPENSES − Product 1		
8. Advertising	_____	_____
9. Sales Promotion	_____	_____
10. Dist. Imprv.	_____	_____
11. Bonus Cost	_____	_____
12. R & D	_____	_____
13. Total Exp. Product 1	_____	_____
14. Project Contribution of Prod. 1 (Line 3 − Line 13)	_____	_____
EXPENSES − Product 2		
15. Advertising	_____	_____
16. Sales Promotion	_____	_____
17. Dist. Imprv.	_____	_____
18. Bonus Cost	_____	_____
19. R & D	_____	_____
20. Total Exp. Product 2	_____	_____
21. Project Contribution of Prod. 2 (Line 6 − Line 20)	_____	_____
22. Gross Contrib./both prod. (Line 14 + Line 21)	_____	_____
OVERHEAD		
23. Sales Force Expenses	_____	_____
24. Sales Force Bonus	_____	_____
25. Inventory Expense	_____	_____
26. Marketing Research	_____	_____
27. Administrative Expense	_____	_____
28. Other Expenses	_____	_____
29. Total Overhead Expenses	_____	_____
30. Net Contribution (Line 22 − Line 29)	_____	_____

FORM 8: MARKETING MIX FACTORS AS A PERCENTAGE OF SALES

COMPANY NO. _____ PERIOD NO. _____

PREPARED BY _____

1. ADVERTISING AS A % OF SALES

$$\frac{\text{Advertising (Product 1)}}{\text{Sales \$ (Product 1)}} = \text{_____} = \text{_____} \%$$

$$\frac{\text{Advertising (Product 2)}}{\text{Sales \$ (Product 2)}} = \text{_____} = \text{_____} \%$$

2. PROMOTION AS A % OF SALES

$$\frac{\text{Sales promotion (Product 1)}}{\text{Sales \$ (Product 1)}} = \text{_____} = \text{_____} \%$$

$$\frac{\text{Sales promotion (Product 2)}}{\text{Sales \$ (Product 2)}} = \text{_____} = \text{_____} \%$$

3. RESEARCH & DEVELOPMENT AS A % OF SALES

$$\frac{\text{R \& D (Product 1)}}{\text{Sales \$ (Product 1)}} = \text{_____} = \text{_____} \%$$

$$\frac{\text{R \& D (Product 2)}}{\text{Sales \$ (Product 2)}} = \text{_____} = \text{_____} \%$$

4. AVERAGE SALES PER SALESPERSON

$$\frac{\text{Sales (Products 1 \& 2)}}{\text{\# salespersons in field}} = \text{_____} = \text{_____} \%$$

5. MARKETING RESEARCH AS A % OF SALES

$$\frac{\text{Marketing research \$}}{\text{Sales \$ (Products 1 \& 2)}} = \text{_____} = \text{_____} \%$$

6. ADMINISTRATIVE EXPENSE AS A % OF SALES

$$\frac{\text{Administrative expense}}{\text{Sales \$ (Products 1 \& 2)}} = \text{_____} = \text{_____} \%$$

FORM 8: MARKETING MIX FACTORS AS A PERCENTAGE OF SALES

COMPANY NO. _____ PERIOD NO. _____

PREPARED BY _____

1. ADVERTISING AS A % OF SALES

$$\frac{\text{Advertising (Product 1)}}{\text{Sales \$ (Product 1)}} = \underline{\hspace{2cm}} = \underline{\hspace{2cm}} \%$$

$$\frac{\text{Advertising (Product 2)}}{\text{Sales \$ (Product 2)}} = \underline{\hspace{2cm}} = \underline{\hspace{2cm}} \%$$

2. PROMOTION AS A % OF SALES

$$\frac{\text{Sales promotion (Product 1)}}{\text{Sales \$ (Product 1)}} = \underline{\hspace{2cm}} = \underline{\hspace{2cm}} \%$$

$$\frac{\text{Sales promotion (Product 2)}}{\text{Sales \$ (Product 2)}} = \underline{\hspace{2cm}} = \underline{\hspace{2cm}} \%$$

3. RESEARCH & DEVELOPMENT AS A % OF SALES

$$\frac{\text{R \& D (Product 1)}}{\text{Sales \$ (Product 1)}} = \underline{\hspace{2cm}} = \underline{\hspace{2cm}} \%$$

$$\frac{\text{R \& D (Product 2)}}{\text{Sales \$ (Product 2)}} = \underline{\hspace{2cm}} = \underline{\hspace{2cm}} \%$$

4. AVERAGE SALES PER SALESPERSON

$$\frac{\text{Sales (Products 1 \& 2)}}{\text{\# salespersons in field}} = \underline{\hspace{2cm}} = \underline{\hspace{2cm}} \%$$

5. MARKETING RESEARCH AS A % OF SALES

$$\frac{\text{Marketing research \$}}{\text{Sales \$ (Products 1 \& 2)}} = \underline{\hspace{2cm}} = \underline{\hspace{2cm}} \%$$

6. ADMINISTRATIVE EXPENSE AS A % OF SALES

$$\frac{\text{Administrative expense}}{\text{Sales \$ (Products 1 \& 2)}} = \underline{\hspace{2cm}} = \underline{\hspace{2cm}} \%$$

FORM 8: MARKETING MIX FACTORS AS A PERCENTAGE OF SALES

COMPANY NO. _____ PERIOD NO. _____

PREPARED BY _____

1. ADVERTISING AS A % OF SALES

$$\frac{\text{Advertising (Product 1)}}{\text{Sales \$ (Product 1)}} = \underline{\hspace{2cm}} = \underline{\hspace{2cm}} \%$$

$$\frac{\text{Advertising (Product 2)}}{\text{Sales \$ (Product 2)}} = \underline{\hspace{2cm}} = \underline{\hspace{2cm}} \%$$

2. PROMOTION AS A % OF SALES

$$\frac{\text{Sales promotion (Product 1)}}{\text{Sales \$ (Product 1)}} = \underline{\hspace{2cm}} = \underline{\hspace{2cm}} \%$$

$$\frac{\text{Sales promotion (Product 2)}}{\text{Sales \$ (Product 2)}} = \underline{\hspace{2cm}} = \underline{\hspace{2cm}} \%$$

3. RESEARCH & DEVELOPMENT AS A % OF SALES

$$\frac{\text{R \& D (Product 1)}}{\text{Sales \$ (Product 1)}} = \underline{\hspace{2cm}} = \underline{\hspace{2cm}} \%$$

$$\frac{\text{R \& D (Product 2)}}{\text{Sales \$ (Product 2)}} = \underline{\hspace{2cm}} = \underline{\hspace{2cm}} \%$$

4. AVERAGE SALES PER SALESPERSON

$$\frac{\text{Sales (Products 1 \& 2)}}{\text{\# salespersons in field}} = \underline{\hspace{2cm}} = \underline{\hspace{2cm}} \%$$

5. MARKETING RESEARCH AS A % OF SALES

$$\frac{\text{Marketing research \$}}{\text{Sales \$ (Products 1 \& 2)}} = \underline{\hspace{2cm}} = \underline{\hspace{2cm}} \%$$

6. ADMINISTRATIVE EXPENSE AS A % OF SALES

$$\frac{\text{Administrative expense}}{\text{Sales \$ (Products 1 \& 2)}} = \underline{\hspace{2cm}} = \underline{\hspace{2cm}} \%$$

FORM 8: MARKETING MIX FACTORS AS A PERCENTAGE OF SALES

COMPANY NO. _____ PERIOD NO. _____

PREPARED BY _____

1. ADVERTISING AS A % OF SALES

$$\frac{\text{Advertising (Product 1)}}{\text{Sales \$ (Product 1)}} = \text{_____} = \text{_____} \%$$

$$\frac{\text{Advertising (Product 2)}}{\text{Sales \$ (Product 2)}} = \text{_____} = \text{_____} \%$$

2. PROMOTION AS A % OF SALES

$$\frac{\text{Sales promotion (Product 1)}}{\text{Sales \$ (Product 1)}} = \text{_____} = \text{_____} \%$$

$$\frac{\text{Sales promotion (Product 2)}}{\text{Sales \$ (Product 2)}} = \text{_____} = \text{_____} \%$$

3. RESEARCH & DEVELOPMENT AS A % OF SALES

$$\frac{\text{R \& D (Product 1)}}{\text{Sales \$ (Product 1)}} = \text{_____} = \text{_____} \%$$

$$\frac{\text{R \& D (Product 2)}}{\text{Sales \$ (Product 2)}} = \text{_____} = \text{_____} \%$$

4. AVERAGE SALES PER SALESPERSON

$$\frac{\text{Sales (Products 1 \& 2)}}{\text{\# salespersons in field}} = \text{_____} = \text{_____} \%$$

5. MARKETING RESEARCH AS A % OF SALES

$$\frac{\text{Marketing research \$}}{\text{Sales \$ (Products 1 \& 2)}} = \text{_____} = \text{_____} \%$$

6. ADMINISTRATIVE EXPENSE AS A % OF SALES

$$\frac{\text{Administrative expense}}{\text{Sales \$ (Products 1 \& 2)}} = \text{_____} = \text{_____} \%$$

FORM 9: DECISION FORM

COMPANY NO. _____ PERIOD NO. _____

INDUSTRY _____

PRODUCT 1:
1. PRODUCTS ORDERED   _____
2. PRICE $ _____
3. ADVERTISING $ _____ ,000
4. SALES PROMOTION $ _____ ,000
5. DISTRIBUTION IMPRV. $ _____ ,000
6. BONUS PAID (per unit) $ _____
7. R & D $ _____ ,000

PRODUCT 2:
8. PRODUCTS ORDERED   _____
9. PRICE $ _____
10. ADVERTISING $ _____ ,000
11. SALES PROMOTION $ _____ ,000
12. DISTRIBUTION IMPRV. $ _____ ,000
13. BONUS PAID (per unit) $ _____
14. R & D $ _____ ,000
15. SALESPERSON CHANGE (+ or –)   _____
16. MARKET RESEARCH #   _____
17. MARKET RESEARCH #   _____
18. MARKET RESEARCH #   _____
19. MARKET RESEARCH #   _____
20. INCIDENT RESPONSE #   _____

VERIFICATION TOTAL   [_____]

Note: Use *whole numbers* only — do not use decimals anyplace. Add all the numbers that you have inserted from item 1 through item 20. Place total in the verification box (do not add the preprinted 000s). This is used to verify the correctness of the numbers as they are typed into the computer. This total *must* be correct or you will be fined. Place a zero in any blank not used but leave Product 2 blanks empty if you are not selling Product 2.

FORM 9: DECISION FORM

COMPANY NO. _____ PERIOD NO. _____

INDUSTRY _____

PRODUCT 1: 1. PRODUCTS ORDERED   _____
             2. PRICE $ _____
             3. ADVERTISING $ _____ ,000
             4. SALES PROMOTION $ _____ ,000
             5. DISTRIBUTION IMPRV. $ _____ ,000
             6. BONUS PAID (per unit) $ _____
             7. R & D $ _____ ,000

PRODUCT 2: 8. PRODUCTS ORDERED   _____
             9. PRICE $ _____
           10. ADVERTISING $ _____ ,000
           11. SALES PROMOTION $ _____ ,000
           12. DISTRIBUTION IMPRV. $ _____ ,000
           13. BONUS PAID (per unit) $ _____
           14. R & D $ _____ ,000
           15. SALESPERSON CHANGE (+ or –)   _____
           16. MARKET RESEARCH #   _____
           17. MARKET RESEARCH #   _____
           18. MARKET RESEARCH #   _____
           19. MARKET RESEARCH #   _____
           20. INCIDENT RESPONSE #   _____

VERIFICATION TOTAL   [_____]

Note: Use *whole numbers* only — do not use decimals anyplace. Add all the numbers that you have inserted from item 1 through item 20. Place total in the verification box (do not add the preprinted 000s). This is used to verify the correctness of the numbers as they are typed into the computer. This total *must* be correct or you will be fined. Place a zero in any blank not used but leave Product 2 blanks empty if you are not selling Product 2.

FORM 9: DECISION FORM

COMPANY NO. _____ PERIOD NO. _____

INDUSTRY _____

PRODUCT 1:   1. PRODUCTS ORDERED   _____

                    2. PRICE $ _____

                    3. ADVERTISING $ _____ ,000

                    4. SALES PROMOTION $ _____ ,000

                    5. DISTRIBUTION IMPRV. $ _____ ,000

                    6. BONUS PAID (per unit) $ _____

                    7. R & D $ _____ ,000

PRODUCT 2:   8. PRODUCTS ORDERED   _____

                    9. PRICE $ _____

                   10. ADVERTISING $ _____ ,000

                   11. SALES PROMOTION $ _____ ,000

                   12. DISTRIBUTION IMPRV. $ _____ ,000

                   13. BONUS PAID (per unit) $ _____

                   14. R & D $ _____ ,000

                   15. SALESPERSON CHANGE (+ or −)   _____

                   16. MARKET RESEARCH #   _____

                   17. MARKET RESEARCH #   _____

                   18. MARKET RESEARCH #   _____

                   19. MARKET RESEARCH #   _____

                   20. INCIDENT RESPONSE #   _____

VERIFICATION TOTAL   [_____]

Note: Use *whole numbers* only — do not use decimals anyplace. Add all the numbers that you have inserted from item 1 through item 20. Place total in the verification box (do not add the preprinted 000s). This is used to verify the correctness of the numbers as they are typed into the computer. This total *must* be correct or you will be fined. Place a zero in any blank not used but leave Product 2 blanks empty if you are not selling Product 2.

FORM 9: DECISION FORM

COMPANY NO. _____ PERIOD NO. _____

INDUSTRY _____

PRODUCT 1: 1. PRODUCTS ORDERED   _____

2. PRICE $ _____

3. ADVERTISING $ _____ ,000

4. SALES PROMOTION $ _____ ,000

5. DISTRIBUTION IMPRV. $ _____ ,000

6. BONUS PAID (per unit) $ _____

7. R & D $ _____ ,000

PRODUCT 2: 8. PRODUCTS ORDERED   _____

9. PRICE $ _____

10. ADVERTISING $ _____ ,000

11. SALES PROMOTION $ _____ ,000

12. DISTRIBUTION IMPRV. $ _____ ,000

13. BONUS PAID (per unit) $ _____

14. R & D $ _____ ,000

15. SALESPERSON CHANGE (+ or −)   _____

16. MARKET RESEARCH #   _____

17. MARKET RESEARCH #   _____

18. MARKET RESEARCH #   _____

19. MARKET RESEARCH #   _____

20. INCIDENT RESPONSE #   _____

VERIFICATION TOTAL   [   ]

Note: Use *whole numbers* only — do not use decimals anyplace. Add all the numbers that you have inserted from item 1 through item 20. Place total in the verification box (do not add the preprinted 000s). This is used to verify the correctness of the numbers as they are typed into the computer. This total *must* be correct or you will be fined. Place a zero in any blank not used but leave Product 2 blanks empty if you are not selling Product 2.

FORM 9: DECISION FORM

COMPANY NO. _____ PERIOD NO. _____

INDUSTRY _____

PRODUCT 1: 1. PRODUCTS ORDERED   _____
            2. PRICE $ _____
            3. ADVERTISING $ _____ ,000
            4. SALES PROMOTION $ _____ ,000
            5. DISTRIBUTION IMPRV. $ _____ ,000
            6. BONUS PAID (per unit) $ _____
            7. R & D $ _____ ,000

PRODUCT 2: 8. PRODUCTS ORDERED   _____
            9. PRICE $ _____
           10. ADVERTISING $ _____ ,000
           11. SALES PROMOTION $ _____ ,000
           12. DISTRIBUTION IMPRV. $ _____ ,000
           13. BONUS PAID (per unit) $ _____
           14. R & D $ _____ ,000
           15. SALESPERSON CHANGE (+ or −) _____
           16. MARKET RESEARCH #   _____
           17. MARKET RESEARCH #   _____
           18. MARKET RESEARCH #   _____
           19. MARKET RESEARCH #   _____
           20. INCIDENT RESPONSE #   _____

           VERIFICATION TOTAL   [   ]

Note: Use *whole numbers* only — do not use decimals anyplace. Add all the numbers that you have inserted from item 1 through item 20. Place total in the verification box (do not add the preprinted 000s). This is used to verify the correctness of the numbers as they are typed into the computer. This total *must* be correct or you will be fined. Place a zero in any blank not used but leave Product 2 blanks empty if you are not selling Product 2.

FORM 9: DECISION FORM

COMPANY NO. _____ PERIOD NO. _____

INDUSTRY _____

PRODUCT 1:
    1. PRODUCTS ORDERED   _____
    2. PRICE $ _____
    3. ADVERTISING $ _____ ,000
    4. SALES PROMOTION $ _____ ,000
    5. DISTRIBUTION IMPRV. $ _____ ,000
    6. BONUS PAID (per unit) $ _____
    7. R & D $ _____ ,000

PRODUCT 2:
    8. PRODUCTS ORDERED   _____
    9. PRICE $ _____
    10. ADVERTISING $ _____ ,000
    11. SALES PROMOTION $ _____ ,000
    12. DISTRIBUTION IMPRV. $ _____ ,000
    13. BONUS PAID (per unit) $ _____
    14. R & D $ _____ ,000
    15. SALESPERSON CHANGE (+ or –) _____
    16. MARKET RESEARCH #   _____
    17. MARKET RESEARCH #   _____
    18. MARKET RESEARCH #   _____
    19. MARKET RESEARCH #   _____
    20. INCIDENT RESPONSE #   _____

VERIFICATION TOTAL   [   ]

Note: Use *whole numbers* only — do not use decimals anyplace. Add all the numbers that you have inserted from item 1 through item 20. Place total in the verification box (do not add the preprinted 000s). This is used to verify the correctness of the numbers as they are typed into the computer. This total *must* be correct or you will be fined. Place a zero in any blank not used but leave Product 2 blanks empty if you are not selling Product 2.

FORM 9: DECISION FORM

COMPANY NO. _____ PERIOD NO. _____

INDUSTRY _____

PRODUCT 1:
1. PRODUCTS ORDERED   _____
2. PRICE $ _____
3. ADVERTISING $ _____ ,000
4. SALES PROMOTION $ _____ ,000
5. DISTRIBUTION IMPRV. $ _____ ,000
6. BONUS PAID (per unit) $ _____
7. R & D $ _____ ,000

PRODUCT 2:
8. PRODUCTS ORDERED   _____
9. PRICE $ _____
10. ADVERTISING $ _____ ,000
11. SALES PROMOTION $ _____ ,000
12. DISTRIBUTION IMPRV. $ _____ ,000
13. BONUS PAID (per unit) $ _____
14. R & D $ _____ ,000
15. SALESPERSON CHANGE (+ or –)   _____
16. MARKET RESEARCH #   _____
17. MARKET RESEARCH #   _____
18. MARKET RESEARCH #   _____
19. MARKET RESEARCH #   _____
20. INCIDENT RESPONSE #   _____

VERIFICATION TOTAL   [_____]

Note: Use *whole numbers* only — do not use decimals anyplace. Add all the numbers that you have inserted from item 1 through item 20. Place total in the verification box (do not add the preprinted 000s). This is used to verify the correctness of the numbers as they are typed into the computer. This total *must* be correct or you will be fined. Place a zero in any blank not used but leave Product 2 blanks empty if you are not selling Product 2.

FORM 9: DECISION FORM

COMPANY NO. _____ PERIOD NO. _____

INDUSTRY _____

PRODUCT 1:   1. PRODUCTS ORDERED   _____

                 2. PRICE $ _____

                 3. ADVERTISING $ _____ ,000

                 4. SALES PROMOTION $ _____ ,000

                 5. DISTRIBUTION IMPRV. $ _____ ,000

                 6. BONUS PAID (per unit) $ _____

                 7. R & D $ _____ ,000

PRODUCT 2:   8. PRODUCTS ORDERED   _____

                 9. PRICE $ _____

               10. ADVERTISING $ _____ ,000

               11. SALES PROMOTION $ _____ ,000

               12. DISTRIBUTION IMPRV. $ _____ ,000

               13. BONUS PAID (per unit) $ _____

               14. R & D $ _____ ,000

               15. SALESPERSON CHANGE (+ or −) _____

               16. MARKET RESEARCH #   _____

               17. MARKET RESEARCH #   _____

               18. MARKET RESEARCH #   _____

               19. MARKET RESEARCH #   _____

               20. INCIDENT RESPONSE #   _____

               VERIFICATION TOTAL   [_____]

Note: Use *whole numbers* only — do not use decimals anyplace. Add all the numbers that you have inserted from item 1 through item 20. Place total in the verification box (do not add the preprinted 000s). This is used to verify the correctness of the numbers as they are typed into the computer. This total *must* be correct or you will be fined. Place a zero in any blank not used but leave Product 2 blanks empty if you are not selling Product 2.